Reviews of *Depression is a Choice*
by A. B. Curtiss

...takes on head first the causes of depression...what it is and how it affects us, and how we can control it...
Newbookreviews.com

...can you shake this negative mood? Yes....fight back by shifting your brain into high gear.
Self Magazine

Excellent work, highly recommended.
The Electric Bookstore

...we literally disconnect the message that we are depressed from one part of the brain to another...
Chicago Tribune

NEVER read a more profound discussion on this topic.
Zoloft Message Board

When you come out of depression, it is like being reborn into a bright, new world...
Human Resource Magazine

...suffered deep depression for twelve years...more than three years since I read Depression is a Choice*....I am cured of my depression.*

Daliah. Rainone, amazon.com

I've been through it all — drugs, drugs, drugs, more drugs, therapy, drugs, more therapy, group therapy, workbooks, books, drugs, and drugs. After 30 years of depression, this book HELPED.

S. F. Reader, amazon.com

Excellent way to re-think your depression...

Robert P. Tema, amazon.com

...culminating healer of my lifelong depression...this book empowered me....No more pills after about 45 years of pills... so grateful.

Barbara L.

...requires a certain vigilance and effort...but...worth it.

Adam Swartz, amazon.com

Great techniques for L.L.D. (Late Life Depression).

ElMera Kelley, Gerontologist

BrainSwitch
out of Depression

Break the Cycle of Despair

To a fellow traveler
ABCurtiss

It is inconceivable to me that anyone would be successful in understanding, much less treating depression, without some knowledge of the small area in the neocortex called the "feelings receptor station." I call it the FRS factor of depression.

— A. B. Curtiss

BrainSwitch

out of Depression

Break the Cycle of Despair

A. B. CURTISS

Healthworks Clinic Press
San Diego, California

ISBN-13   978-0-932529-54-2

Printed in the United States of America.

Library of Congress Cataloging-in-Publication Data
Curtiss, A. B.
Brainswitching: conquering the demon of depression/ A. B. Curtiss.
cm.
ISBN 0-932529-54-2
1. Depression, Mental 2. Depression, Mental—alternative treatment.
3. Curtiss, A. B. I. Title
RC537 . C875 2007   616. 85'27—dc21

10 9 8 7 6 5 4 3 2

To my husband Ray
who fills my life

Contents

Acknowledgments

I would like to thank all those who have encouraged my writing efforts over the years and especially those who found space in their busy lives to help me with reviewing and editing this book. I was fortunate to have among them not only professional writers and editors but in many cases they were, as well, an RN,BSN nurse, a psychiatrist or two, a psychotherapist, a gerontologist, a biologist, a bio-feedback specialist, a scientist, management consultant and human resource specialist. They not only helped catch the typos but were invaluable as a resource to keep my language from going even a hairsbreadth out of line as I crossed disciplines into their area of expertise. If you are not a scientist, for instance, you may just *think* you know what gravity is.

So thanks again to my husband, Ray; my mother, Bert Beman; my sons, Deane, Ford and Wolf Curtiss; my daughters, Demming Forsythe and Sunday Arvidson; my daughters-in-law, Paula Curtiss and Shelli Curtiss; my aunt, Lucy Baukney; my brother, Lewis; my sisters-in-law, Judy Beman and Jeanne Cramer; my brother-in-law, Ed Curtiss; my nephews, Harlan Cramer and Tom Cramer; my cousins,

Debi and Hunter Moss and Barbara Foster who are always enthusiastic supporters of all my efforts.

Thanks also to my friends and associates for their interest in this book and their continuing advice and support: Tom Szasz, Judith Hand, Bob Holt, Bob Goodman, Barbara Villasenor, Barry Friedman, Donna Erickson, Judy Levine, Pete Johnson, Terry and Lynn Badger, Sofia Shafquat, Steve Psomas, Marian Psomas, Bobbi Janikas, Pat Pangburn, Helen Lee Fletcher, Carmen Torrent, Wanda Belmont, Anne Janda, Karen and Cole Black, Olga Seibert, Sue Flannery, Jeff and Maria Edwards, Sandy McVey, Kelsey McVey, Elizabeth Tovsrud, Loretta Strang, Nat Lehrman, Tom Nolan, Bob Brady, John Winston Bush, Mera Kelly, Sally Lee Hunter, Jack Levis, Bob and Susan Fisher, Walt and Linnea Notton, Judy and Taylor Hines, Nick Wright, Ward and Vera Wright, Jon and Cris Fleming, Pete Engels, Bonnie Robison, Nira Brand, Mim Rutz, Pete and Betty Demming, Rosie & Bob Stubbs, Bun and Bill Wood, Ashley Jansen, Ursula Sweeney, Marianne and Dave Forward, Jake and Jane Jacobsen, Jim and Mary Jacobsen, Dave and CeeCee Wainwright, and R. Lee Hammett.

One

What You've Always Needed to Know about Depression

When you know its working parts, depression will no longer suck you in like a sinking star.

Depression once brought me to my knees. It was the fight of my life. I won that fight and so can you! Most people who seek help for depression want to know two things: Is there something that can stop the torture? And can I do it without drugs? The answer is yes, and yes. All suffering, depression included, can be and should be understood in the larger terms of utilizing *healthy brain functions*, not just brain pathology.

You have probably opened this book because you or someone you love is struggling with depression. You have come to the right place. I am a licensed cognitive behavioral therapist and a certified hypnotist. I worked in a woman's counseling center for seven years before I opened my own private practice. One of the most important things in my background is that as a young woman in my thirties I was diagnosed with manic-depression, as was my father and brother. It's now called bipolar disorder but I prefer the original term for its more graphic description.

Although I am a happy person now, for almost 30 years I was an unhappy one. Chronic depression devastated my life, and almost ruined my marriage. In the last fifteen years I have been so little troubled by depression that I no longer think of it as the enemy of the spirit so much as the teacher of the soul.

Not that depression doesn't still come down upon me. I spent so many years being depressed that those neural patterns are practically hardwired in my brain. However, when they are triggered for whatever reason, *I am out of them in minutes instead of the days, weeks, or months it used to take.* Depression no longer has the power to interrupt my life because I know what to do when it attacks.

Depression can happen to anyone

Perfectly normal people can have depression, anxiety, and panic attacks. They may come on suddenly and unexpectedly; or they can be your constant companion for weeks, months, or even years. The pain can be so unbearable that some people even consider ending it all just to escape it.

Sometimes depression occurs when things are going well and there's no clear reason for our sudden unhappiness. At other times depression and problems become so inter-mixed that we think we are suffering from our problems when, in fact, we are suffering from our depression.

The symptoms are not going away by themselves anytime soon. Even though depression is certainly cyclical, you can't count on its cyclical nature to enable depression to cure itself. But a new cognitive behavior technique called "Brainswitching" uses the principles underlying its cyclic nature to rescue you quickly from the agony of depression. Depression is like living in a room of pain; you can learn how to leave the room.

You cannot will yourself out of a deep depression because the pain is caused by a chemical imbalance. But this targeted system of mind techniques can short-circuit the agony by disconnecting the message that you are depressed from one part of the brain to the other until the chemical balance is restored. Brainswitching deals instantly with the physical pain of depression. Cognitive behavior therapy and psychotherapy do not. Drugs may take weeks or months to work.

However, it will not take you long to learn Brainswitching. Those who get depressed know how rapidly we can be laid low by it. Now here is a process that can get us out of it just as fast. It's about time! Until now depression has been an unsolvable problem for millions of people.

Two different schools of thinking about depression

To add to our confusion, two entirely different schools of thought about depression have been polarizing in the last few years providing little security in the middle for those looking for a safe and sure treatment that really works.

Chronic depression has become like the old proverb: *Who shall decide when doctors disagree?* Meanwhile people's very lives are hanging in the balance.

One thinking insists depression is a character flaw or psychological problem that's "all in your head." The solutions that come along with this theory tend to be low-key, sporadic, and non-specific. It suggests that you do such things as count your blessings and be grateful for what you have, exercise more emotional self-control, think positive, take the bad along with the good like everybody else, plan a weekly pleasant activity, take up jogging, volunteer to help others less fortunate, accept your pain and it will disappear.

The other school of thought claims just the opposite, that depression *definitely* is not "all in your head." This theory holds depression to be an incurable, genetically-based mental illness, over which you have *no control whatsoever.* The treatment advocated here is therapy and medication for the rest of your life.

This dichotomy has not only been a problem for those who are depressed, but for the professional community dedicated to helping them. Our common sense need not be trapped any longer in this therapeutic tug of war. There is a better answer!

The FRS factor of depression

We need to understand that depression is more than an incomplete gestalt of self-reported symptoms. We need to treat depression more than palliatively. We need to understand and treat depression neuroscientifically for the *biochemical* event that it is. *This is not incompatible with either school of thought,* and it successfully addresses the legitimate concerns of both.

This was the subject of my workshops for the California Council on Family Relations. The conference was mostly attended by students, counselors, and psychologists whose careers involve helping people through their emotional setbacks.

My lectures included an explanation of the physiological components of our feelings—*how* do we feel what we feel? I discussed the process whereby signals from the emotional part of the brain (the subcortex) must travel upwards and be acknowledged in the thinking part of the brain (the neocortex) before a human being is able to feel any pain or emotion.

It is inconceivable to me that anyone would be successful in understanding, *much less treating depression*, without some knowledge of the small area in the neocortex called the "feelings receptor station." I call it the FRS factor of depression. But when I asked the mainly professional audience if they had ever heard of this neuronal process of pain perception before, not a single hand went up!

Of course it is such a tiny event, brain-wise, that it happens beneath our level of awareness. But this small instantaneous process underlies the reason depression is cyclical. The fact that depression is cyclical is extremely important. All depression ends at some point, sooner or later, *anyway*. Why not move it faster along its natural continuum and get it to end sooner, rather than later? This is the whole point of Brainswitching.

Once aware of the pain perception process in the neocortex, we can take advantage of it to move ourselves out of depression rapidly. Much faster than would be the normal course of any depressive event. You can get so good at Brainswitching that depression will cease to be a major issue in your life. You can opt out of it quickly whenever it strikes.

First, you need to know a little bit about how your brain works

Brainswitching is not a magic bullet. You have to do a little work before you get the hang of it. Nevertheless, the same way that many diabetics can stem the tide of their disease with slight changes in their diet and exercise, those with depression can turn their whole life around by making small, precise, and particular interruptions in certain habitual thinking processes. If you don't understand this last sentence, don't worry. The first few chapters will make it crystal clear.

In order to make these changes, you will need a bare-bones education in how your brain functions which you will get in the beginning chapters of this book. Don't be alarmed. All you really need to know about your brain can be understood by any serious-minded eighth-grader. And you will be a wiser, more tranquil person for your effort.

With this information you can make use of the latest research which shows that depression, anxiety, and even obsessive-compulsive disorders can be eliminated by altering one or two thinking patterns. You can sidetrack automatic depressive patterns by building new and more helpful *get-out-of-depression* patterns which you soon learn to use as automatically as the old destructive ones. Again, how to do this will become clear as you read the book.

As a psychotherapist I endured lengthy bouts of life-dulling depression for decades. Not anymore! I discovered the mechanism behind Brainswitching in cutting-edge neuroscience research and brain-mapping as I strove to help those who came into my counseling office looking for relief from their pain. As a result I found the answer to my own chronic depression, mania, anxiety, and panic attacks that I had struggled with for so long.

You can side-step depression

I have successfully presented my research findings to the National Board of Cognitive Behavioral Therapists and subsequently have provided workshops for professional organizations and holistic health schools. Thousands of people are now learning the technique.

Brainswitching is immediate. It lets you quickly side-step the depression which is generated in the emotional part of your brain (the subcortex) by taking temporary refuge in the thinking part of your brain (the neocortex), *which never contains depression*. Brainswitching handles stress, anxiety, and depression from the feelings receptor station in the neocortex.

The process allows you to consciously shift the neuronal activity of your brain from the subcortex, where depression is always located, to the neocortex which does not have the capacity for depression. You can learn to do this.

Brainswitching is for you if you have any kind of recurring depression or anxiety; if you have felt vaguely disconnected and too stressed to have the normal life that you see other people enjoying; or if you have asked yourself the question: "Will I ever be really happy again?"

Brainswitching short-circuits the short circuit

There's no doubt that depression, or indeed any serious emotional upset, has the capacity to temporarily short-circuit the thinking brain. Suddenly we are under stress. We are anxious, or depressed, and we can't think straight. Our mind seems to go blank, and our normal thinking goes "off line."

There is good reason for this. The emotional brain, being the ancient core system around which all the rest of the brain subsequently evolved, is our primal instinct. We are genetically scripted to get automatically hooked by it. However, once you have a "bird's eye view" of how the whole system operates, you will become more wary of getting snagged in it. You will be able to by-pass this emotional short-circuit, and access your thinking brain again. That is the subject of this book.

Depression is real. We can feel it. Hook us up to a brain scan and we can see it. We can measure it in the lost hours and lost opportunities of our lives. We can quantify it chemically, bioelectrically, and neuroscientifically. We can verify it physically and psychologically. And now, thankfully, we can stop it with Brainswitching.

Two

You *Can* Get out of the Torture Chamber

The most difficult problem often has the simplest solution.

Deep in my brain there still exists this neural torture chamber into which my mind periodically throws me. Down, down I sink into the blackness. I hear the sickening click of the lock behind me. I am paralyzed with fear. There are no windows to see out of this pain. I am trapped, lost! Who will help me? I am beyond help, beyond hope. The agony! The agony! I cannot stand the pain.

But then I remember! I have the key out of this terrible place right here in my pocket. It's called Brainswitching. I don't have to stay here. I can immediately begin to free myself. Of course I could not do this in the beginning, just as you or your loved one cannot do it now. But be assured. Anyone can *learn* to do it.

I sought help for depression

As a young woman I was successful in many other aspects of my life. So I couldn't understand why I was often filled with such debilitating hopelessness that I couldn't get out of bed for days; that I would cry for hours; that in the midst of my loving family I would feel nothing but the pain of isolated loneliness.

People who have never suffered from depression and want us to "snap out of it" have no idea of that unbearable agony. I went from doctor to doctor hoping for a better solution. Finally I stopped going to psychotherapists and became one.

I went back to graduate school. It was here that I finally found out what was the matter with me. I was completely ignorant of how my own brain functioned and how my nervous system worked. The dirty little secret is that if our brain feels bad, it is because we have unknowingly *given it instructions* to feel bad.

We simply don't know how the darn thing works. And, like any extremely complex machinery, if we don't know how the brain works we can bumble around pushing all the wrong buttons, causing malfunctions like chemical imbalance.

What you don't know can't help you

With some knowledge, we can push the *right* buttons. But without some tools of understanding, when you are deep into depression, you cannot reach far enough into yourself to rescue your heart from its own dark cave. I have already spent too much time in such a dark cave myself.

Although I still may be instantly hurled there on occasion, I now make my visits extremely short. I no longer take up residence in that painful chaos of mind. How do I manage that? I have learned exactly how my brain produces depression, and precisely how I can put a stop to it.

Depression is the only pain that remembers. It not only remembers, it recreates itself over, and over, and over. In a way it is the ultimate post-traumatic stress syndrome. The physical pain, the psychological fear, the feelings of worthlessness, helplessness, and despair are all bound up and entangled in a neural pattern that takes on a life of its own, seemingly independent of our will. I say *seemingly* because we usually are not aware that we focus our attention *away* from our will at this time. We focus only on the depressive pattern. We can learn not to do this.

A new way of thinking is the answer

Since the pain of depression is recurring and virtually unchanging, second-guessing can become your best strategy. As you are able to anticipate the repetitive nature of what happens, you can now practice and correct your responses ahead of time. This way you can continually sharpen your wits against what depression throws at you. As powerful as it is, you will begin to see that it is a lifeless old syndrome that can't create new possibilities for itself. But *you* can; with Brainswitching!

Brainswitching can disconnect you from the depressive neural pattern and build another neural pattern as a bridge to your rational faculties. You can almost immediately connect to your regular world again. It may be a new idea to you that you can build a neural pattern in your brain as an act of will; but this is what we do anytime that we acquire a new skill or habit.

I realize now that I was never depressed because I was *sick*. I was depressed because I was *wrong*. Depression easily misleads us, by the overwhelming fear and physical agony of it, into believing that we have nothing within us to fall back on. We are trapped in a death-like emptiness. We can't concentrate. The things we used to take pleasure in suddenly have no meaning. We believe we have lost the capacity to think, feel, and enjoy the way we used to.

This is never true. Not a single bit of our extremely complex mind ever disappears or "goes blank" because of our moods. Just the opposite. It is our moods that flare up and then go blank. With all its creativity, reason, and intelligence, with all its capacity for ongoingness, our whole mind remains completely intact and *immediately available* to us even in the depths of depression. We simply must learn how to properly access it at this difficult time.

Getting stuck in depression is a learned response

Getting out of depression is a learned skill that millions of people have accomplished. They've probably picked up coping mechanisms and mind techniques as children that they are completely unaware of. The only thing they know is that they don't get depressed "like other people."

The millions of people who *do* suffer from depression don't know these simple but important skills. To acquire them as adults involves some restructuring of thinking habits. More conscious and intellectual effort is needed. Again, don't worry. The exercises are simple.

The exercises help us learn the difference between being responsible *to* our mind and being responsible *for* our mind. When we are responsible *to* our mind it's like being responsible to our parents or our teacher, or our boss. We have to do what they want no matter how foolish we think it is.

It's the same way with our minds. When we are responsible *to* our mind we think we must go along with whatever raging emotional upset, despair, or anxiety might be triggering up in the neurons of our brain. Instead, we can learn to be responsible *for* our mind. We can direct the neurons to do the kind of thinking that will be helpful to us instead of harmful.

We can't use hope and a sense of fulfillment *to get rid* of depression. Our brains do not work that way. Depression is a biochemical event. It needs a biochemical solution. But this does not necessarily mean pharmaceutical drugs.

Depression loses its power

Thanks to Brainswitching, the hopeless anguish that was once the most real thing in my life no longer holds power over me. I can see depression for what it is—a temporary mind construction caused by a chemical imbalance in the brain. And I know how to dismantle it quickly, using the same building blocks by which it arose.

It took me several years to develop this small, precise expertise. It is replicable. I can teach it to you. It can be used to supplement any other methods you are now using for depression. It has no negative side effects. Brainswitching can absolutely pull you out of any depressive episode. It takes immediate action to thwart the biochemical imbalance that causes all the pain.

You don't have to be a psychotherapist, or some kind of heroic person to do Brainswitching. You can be just an ordinary human being, frantic and frightened like I once was, and thinking you will never be a normal happy person again. I assure you, you can be!

Anybody can do this

Sometimes I have been criticized by people who say, "Well sure, *you* can get out of depression because you are a *therapist*." My answer is that maybe special training is necessary to research and synthesize psychological information into a working process. But once the process is created, anyone can use it. In this respect, Brainswitching is like the game of Checkers. Perhaps it takes special knowledge to *invent it*, but once it's invented, even a child can learn to play it.

I relate my early journey out of depression in a book called *Depression is a Choice: Winning the Battle Without Drugs*. It is a more philosophical book than this one, a memoir of how I got out of manic-depression without the customary orthodox drug treatment. By the way, the title was my publisher's idea. My choice of title was *The Woman Who Traded Her Mind for a Green Frog*. "Green Frog" is the name of the first Brainswitching exercise I ever used.

Brainswitching and Directed Thinking have worked for thousands of people who have read my first book and visited my web site, www.depressionisachoice.com. Brainswitching is a specific kind of Directed Thinking. One man emailed me, "Before Directed Thinking I never fully understood mindfulness, meditation, or what it was like to really live in the NOW." Another wrote, "The best thing I learned from your book is the awareness of my awareness."

Professor of Psychology Dr. Al Infande wrote me that *Depression is a Choice* "has to be one the best books I have ever read on the topic of depression. And I mean it! Your book made more sense about the concept of depression than any other book I ever read."

Why did I write a second book?

So many readers of my earlier work suggested that a how-to book with more mind exercises would be a helpful addition to the memoir. Also, I get letters all the time from people desperate for some step-by-step, practical way out of depression, either for themselves or for someone they love. Letters like this:

Our 23-year old daughter has been diagnosed with bipolar disorder. The doctors tell her that her condition is incurable, and that she will need to be on a combination of medication and therapy for the rest of her life. We are desperate. We finally came across your web site and everything you suggest on your depression web site is just the opposite from what our daughter is doing.

She is on sick leave, so she is not working. She is not involved in anything constructive. She is not exercising at all, and has nothing but time on her hands to dwell on her depression, which I can see is only making her worse. She is very self-absorbed and her therapy keeps her dwelling on her past and what she may have experienced, instead of on today and what she can do. Can you recommend a therapist in our area that uses your techniques of Directed Thinking? We think it makes so much sense, and it has given us our first ray of hope.

Free from depression

When I was first diagnosed with depression I was convinced that I did nothing to cause the hopeless despair that periodically laid me low. I didn't think I could do anything to fix it either. Now I know better. When depression strikes, I take over. I am the one in charge, not my rampaging emotions. Of course, in order to do this, it helps to know something about how your brain works!

All depressed people think we have a problem with our feelings, with our chemical neurotransmitters such as serotonin. True. But more importantly we have a problem with our *thinking* about our feelings. Most of our pain is caused by what we are thinking and doing and we can think and do *something else.*

One of our major problems is that we have been sensitized by stress to over-react to our feelings. Depression is more of a geometric than an arithmetic progression. It's a reaction to the stress of the reaction to the stress of the reaction to the stress of the reaction ad infinitum, each progression producing more chemical imbalance and thus more pain.

Depression dissolves when self-debilitating mindsets are changed

Depression is a *place* in the brain we get to. We don't have to stay there. We get there by thinking a certain way, which causes a chemical imbalance. And we can get out by thinking a different way, which will correct the chemical imbalance.

When I say depression is a thinking problem I do not mean this terrible feeling is *imaginary.* Far from it! It is basic body chemistry. It is physically excruciating to the point where some people have even thought of ending it all, or actually tried to. But it is a needless tragedy because there is a solution.

If only I had known in my younger years what I know now, my life would have been so much better. But then I wouldn't have become a therapist either, and perhaps my life would have lacked some depth as well. It is probably better to have borne adversity and conquered, rather than never to have suffered at all. Certainly without the adversity of my own depression, I couldn't have written this book.

Brainswitching works for any kind of depression. Depression is not quantitative; it is a qualitative state of being. It is a state of alarm. Most people think of depression as a mood, but neuroscientifically speaking it is caused by a neural thinking *mode*. Therefore, even those who are deep into depression can recover the same as someone with a milder case. When you change the manner of thinking that caused it, the chemical imbalance fades, and the despair goes away. No matter what was the gradation of despair, gone is gone!

First you have to learn some basic biology

The next few chapters will discuss all the information you will need about how your brain works: the two main parts of the brain; how you get, neuroscientifically speaking, from one thought to another; the two different kinds of thinking that human beings all do (one of which leads to depression); the role of the psychological defense system; and the chemical consequences of the triggering of the fight-or-flight response. This is necessary so you can understand the mind exercises that follow.

The mind exercises are all very simple; anybody can do them. They require no preparatory techniques or previous knowledge other than what you read here. They promote a sense of well-being and calm. For one thing, at least while you're doing them you are not punishing yourself with guilt about your depression. The decision to do some small good thing for yourself can be the starting point of a complete turnabout in your feelings.

These exercises are not only for beginners but for those familiar with the new human potential training, neuro-linguistic programming, and ACT (Acceptance and Commitment Therapy). They will find much here that is new.

They are wonderful for children too. Just as we give them toys that teach color, distance, and balance, these exercises teach the thinking part of the brain to calm the over-emotional part.

Exercises teach you how to DO *calm* in order to BE *calm*

You cannot cause a brain state (a phenomenal state) to appear by simply knowing something, or wanting something, or setting up the outside circumstances of your life although that is the first step. Many people think that happiness is somehow caused by circumstances other than their own thinking. This is not true. Lottery winners, plucked from otherwise disastrous fates by Lady Luck, seldom maintain their sense of well-being. And normal people, overwhelmed with sudden tragedy, can regain their inner happiness despite grievous losses.

Our moods are not dictated by our changing fortunes. They are established by our long-standing thinking habits. There is an old saying, "The wages of sin is death." *The wages of habit is more habit.* Whatever life we practice, that's the person we become. To produce calmer thinking instead of our habitual depressive thinking, we have to retrain our brain with exercises the same way we would exercise weak arms and legs to regain proper strength.

If you exercise a muscle, it will become strong. If you exercise a thought, it will become *dominant*. The brain always follows the direction of its most current dominant thought. Unfortunately, in exercising depression for years, many of us allow negative neural thought patterns to build into a destructive dominance. Then we wonder why we get "hooked" into depression. We wonder why we're not happy.

To turn around from that, we must exercise "calm" the same way we exercised "depressed." You can easily begin to do it. The exercises are short and simple. Some take less than 30 seconds.

Knowing is not doing

Mental exercises are important. We don't achieve strong muscles *knowing* how to lift weights. We have to actually lift them. We can't play the guitar or piano, or learn how to type with just the *idea* that this finger goes here and that finger goes there. We have to *practice, practice, practice,* until the neuronal patterns form physically in our brain. This is as true for getting out of depression as it is for learning how to play the piano.

Getting the idea intellectually is not enough. You must experience the idea through mental or physical *action,* which imprints it in a usable mind pattern. If your depression patterns are already well-imprinted because you have been practicing them for a long time, don't worry. By practicing new kinds of thinking, you can form new brain patterns that do not contain the old depression.

Brainswitching exercises

Brainswitching exercises are an efficient first-aid for depression or stress. You can do them when you are jumping out of your skin with anxiety, fear, and guilt; or sunk deep into despair, unable to work or sleep. There are other Directed Thinking exercises that prepare your mind for thinking changes, leading to a more stress-free and anxiety-free existence.

The mind has to help us do all this human thinking and being every day of our lives. Like any other part of us our mind needs to be nourished, soothed, stretched, and strengthened so that it will not be too weak, too frightened, or unresponsive when we call upon it.

Spiritually speaking, some suffering may be necessary for our humanity. But too much suffering can also *separate* us from our humanity. Turning from the negative to the positive, from your pain to your life, is not easy to do. You know it's not easy to do. You've probably already tried to do it. Don't give up on yourself. This book will show you how to do it.

Three

The Human Brain

We can teach our brain to do the kind of thinking
we *want or we can allow our brain to "think us"*
into depression.

First you have to get out of the habit of calling yourself names! You have to peel off the downer labels you have been sticking on your own mental forehead and looking at in the mirror of your mind. And don't let anybody else label you either. The problem is that you can't quit doing something that you don't even realize you're doing. Start to look for it. Maybe you haven't been aware of the name-calling. If you decide to check out your self-talk, you will find it.

As we have learned from those who have survived cancer, defeatist thinking and discouraging labels of illness do not contribute to better health. Cancer patients who focus on a self-image of being ill do not do as well as patients who consistently remind themselves instead, that they are "getting better;" that they are "feeling better."

The point is not to *become* our diagnosis but to recover from it. The quickest way to *become* your diagnosis is to keep calling yourself by it! Recent research has shown us what holistic health has been saying for decades. There is a deep body/mind connection. Your body believes every word you tell yourself. *Think* sick and you will *become* sick. *Think* depressed and you will *get* depressed.

You've probably heard all this mind/body stuff before. The paragraph above seems self-evident. Herein lies the very problem. There are a lot of truths that are self-evident. That's why they get lost to us if we're not careful. Nobody can patent them, manufacture them, or make any money on them. So who is going to prescribe them? In the list of "treatments" for depression, self-evident truths seldom appear. So little importance is attached to self-evident truths that they can sometimes cease being self-evident because they lose their relevance to us.

One of the biggest self-evident truths is that we have to stop thinking of ourselves as being depressed and never think that unhelpful thought again. How do we do that? Here is a very simple exercise. You may think the exercise is silly. But it's not as silly as calling ourselves destructive names. And don't let the simplicity fool you. It is very difficult to do even the simplest mind exercises if you are new to the idea of Directed Thinking and choosing your thoughts on purpose. Just because something is simple does not mean it is easy.

When we are depressed, thinking "I am depressed," like thinking "I have cancer," is the most natural thing in the world. But it does not help our situation. We can train ourselves to quit thinking that thought. This one thing alone

Exercise for Getting Rid of Unhelpful Labels

Choose some nonsense word like yadda-yadda or hippity-hop, or some nursery rhyme phrase like "Hark, hark, the dogs do bark!" Whenever you catch yourself saying "I'm depressed," "I'm bipolar," "I'm unhappy," or any other downer name that you have been calling yourself, immediately substitute the word or nursery rhyme. You will at first go back and forth. "I'm depressed." "Hippity-hop." "I'm depressed." "Hippity-hop." "I'm depressed." "Hippity-hop." But stick with it and pretty soon "Hippity-hop" will become a thinking habit that takes the place of the old labeling habit. And since "Hippity-hop" or any nonsense phrase is a neutral thought, it will not have the same harmful emotional and biochemical effect on the brain. You can always drop the nonsense thought when some other more productive thinking starts to take place. But whenever destructive self-labeling starts up again, substitute the nonsense thought to "thought-jam" the destructive thought and keep it from impacting your mind/body. When you first attempt this exercise, it will seem lame and paltry. In addition to the depression and nonsense-phrase flipping back and forth, there will be the self-fulfilling prophesy that "it isn't working." Treat this negative thought just like the depressive thought and keep on concentrating on the nonsense thought. Then turn your mind to some small chore and start thinking about what you are *doing* and *not* what you are *feeling*.

can make a huge difference in the amount of pain depression normally causes us.

Even after they receive such a diagnosis, it does not help cancer patients to think of their illness as incurable. It does not help us either to think of our depression as an incurable illness of the brain. First of all, many people do beat cancer and millions of people do beat depression. Rather than thinking we are mentally ill, it is better to think that our brain is fine, thank you very much. We just have to learn how to *use it better*. To do that, we must know a little more about our brain.

The human brain

There's no need to label and describe all the parts of our brain in order to connect with it from the position of its manager rather than its slave. Do you not think we are a slave to our brain when we suffer days, weeks, months, even years of depression? Please believe me, this torture is not necessary. You *can* learn to get out of it.

There are many ways to symbolically divide up the brain to study it. Artists better understand themselves by seeing the differences between the right and left hemispheres. Philosophers talk about the higher mind of reason having to wrestle the lower mind of passions. The terms "higher mind" and "lower mind" refer to the more scientific terms neocortex and subcortex.

For purposes of this book we are not so interested in the brain architecturally as *functionally*. It is helpful to recognize the difference between the brain's cognitive and emotional features which are, respectively, located in the upper and lower portions. I like the way neuroscientist Antonio Damasio describes it: "The old brain core handles basic biological regulation down in the basement, while up above, the neocortex deliberates with wisdom and subtlety. Upstairs in the cortex there is reason and willpower, while downstairs in the subcortex there is emotion and all that weak, fleshy stuff."

The two main parts of the brain

Throughout the book we will use the term neocortex to refer to the thinking part of our brain, the upper cognitive portion. The term subcortex will refer to the feeling part of our brain, the lower, emotional portion.

The subcortex is the most ancient part of our brain. It's also called the primal mind, or reptilian brain. Way back in the evolutionary chain, our defense system was nothing more than a "STOP-do-not-go-forward-danger-ahead" instinct. This system became more complex as we developed the neocortex (new brain) which was built on top of, around, and through the subcortex. Evolutionarily speaking, depression is a complex further adaptation of that old "STOP-do-not-go-forward" instinct. And, indeed, depression does accomplish a *stop* in our lives very successfully.

Other basic terms used throughout the book

Concerning the terms "mind" and "brain:" Although the mind can be thought of as the *product* of the brain, in some contexts the terms are *functionally* interchangeable.

Throughout the book, the term "thought" will include any image, word, phrase, or idea.

We will use the general term stress chemicals when referring to adrenalin (epinephrine), norepinephrine, and other hormones concerned with the body expressing stress.

Evolutionarily speaking, the mind is an elaborate defense mechanism

Although it is true that we create art, music, mathematics, and literature with the mind, this is not its bottom-line, fail-safe, core function. Our mind is naturally inclined to revert back to a primal instinctive defense mechanism when we are not actively engaging it in some on-going, goal-driven activity like baking a cake or writing a paper.

If we are not using our mind on purpose, this instinctive defensive mindset emerges *on its own*, stealthily and seamlessly. If we are not aware of this latent, default-mode defensive capacity, we will not understand how we sometimes become anxious and paranoid for "no reason."

This evolutionary, negative and paranoid bent of our mind is not all a bad thing. We need a strong psychological defense mechanism. A tough guardian is supposed to be paranoid. You don't see the secret service men who guard the president of the United States all laid back, joyful, and positive. No. When they are working, they are in a constant state of uneasy vigilance. They are frowning, squinting their eyes looking for trouble, looking for problems, looking for that one-in-a-million something that might go wrong.

To our own mind *we* are the president that must be protected at all cost. To protect us, our mind is always looking for trouble, chasing down the negative, peering into every dusty, dark neuronal corner. That is its job. And it is always on duty, even when we are asleep, or not paying any attention to what we are thinking.

So what does this have to do with depression? When our mind gets too paranoid and anxious, there is a chemical reaction in the brain to this kind of thinking that can skew the chemical balance which is the precursor of depression.

Four

What Actually Causes Depression?

Depression is caused by a chemical imbalance in the brain.

If you are depressed, ipso facto, you have a chemical imbalance in your brain. Depression is the by-product of our human psychological defense system. Our defense system is *activated by fearful or anxious thoughts* which trigger the fight-or-flight response. This causes the production of stress chemicals that biochemically prepare us for immediate action.

The chemical imbalance of depression is caused by the *inadvertent* triggering of the fight-or-flight response which dumps stress chemicals into our brain; chemicals like adrenaline, epinephrine, norepinephrine, etc. It is helpful to understand this process from its evolutionary roots.

It would not have been enough for the caveman just to *see* a tiger in order to leap into action. He had to *fear* the tiger so his body could produce the stress chemicals necessary to biologically *empower* him to action. Modern man has essentially the same system. Fearful thoughts start up the stress-chemical factory in order to biochemically give us immediate energy and strength to either fight or flee our enemy. While this instinctive, automatic system was fine for the caveman, it has often proved a depressive undoing for modern man.

This side of the jungle our high-tech lives are more complex than "see-tiger, throw spear." The result is that our fight-or-flight response can be triggered accidentally by *symbolic* tigers—by stressful thoughts about a business lunch, a computer failure, job loss, a fight with our "ex," a crying baby or just a pile of papers on our desks *that we know to be bills.* The jolt of fear goes through us. The stress chemicals start up.

Living in the NOW

The caveman probably lived his whole life in the NOW, in present reality. We do not. We live a great deal of our daily lives in the past, or worrying about the past projected as future. We know, for instance, many months ahead that the tiger is going to be coming down our path in the form of a tax bill, or some long-term project coming due.

Thanks to our advanced technology we know long before a deadly hurricane or snowstorm will hit. So we can often spend days stuck in some particular worry rut when there is no more practical action we can take. At some point our apprehension may escalate, the fight-or-flight response will trigger, and the stress chemicals will begin to pour into our brains. The fight-or-flight response does not depend upon present reality to be triggered. It is triggered *by our thoughts about reality,* or even fantasy.

This is sad to say, but without a great deal of effort the modern human being can very easily live most of his adult life *figuratively* rather than literally, reacting to his imaginings rather than proactively managing himself and his actual connection to present reality. This certainly is true for people with depression. Why?

This is important to remember. The fight-or-flight system does *not* trigger because we are in a dangerous situation. It triggers because we *think* we are in danger. It is our THOUGHTS that cause our emotions, *NOT REALITY.* In real estate you need to fully understand three words— location, location and location. In depression you need to fully understand three words— perception, perception and perception. We could be in a real life-and-death situation and not realize it, and our fight-or-flight system will not activate. Or, we could be perfectly safe and start feeling anxious, and *off it will go!*

So it is no surprise that depression can occur in the absence of any concrete problems. Depression is a psychological "This is the house that Jack built." This is the anxious thought, that connected with the terrible thought, that sparked up the fearful thought, that branched into two terrible memories, that triggered the fight-or-flight response, that caused the chemical imbalance, that caused the depression.

The following chapters will raise your awareness of the kind of "unconscious" and destructive thinking that puts you on the path to depression. Without such awareness, these depression-precursor thoughts can be rampant without the least suspicion on your part that they are going on. The only thing you realize is that you are starting to feel anxious, then depression suddenly erupts.

The chemical imbalance

How does the chemical imbalance cause depression? When our fight-or-flight response has been triggered and there is no immediate rational action to take, we cannot make good use of the stress chemicals produced. The chemical imbalance that was normalized in the caveman's physical fight with the tiger now stews around in our various organs, including our brain, causing hyper-anxiety.

These unused stress chemicals are extremely hard on the tissues of the body, depleting our metabolic energy. Ultimately we end up in a very weak, helpless, and painful depression. Of course if there is a real tiger in your living room you'll need the chemical imbalance. If not, the syndrome need not be a problem once we understand the situation.

When we short-circuit depression temporarily with Brainswitching, the thinking process that triggered the fight-or-flight response abates and the chemical balance is restored. Excess stress chemicals can be quickly dissipated by physical exercise such as working out in the gym, jogging, yoga, or by doing mental exercises and mind tricks.

Psychological fight-or-flight exercises can right our chemical imbalance because they provide the mind with the same emotional release as the *physical* fight-or-flight action of the caveman. This is because, although *we* may know the difference, the memory system of the brain cannot tell the difference between a *real* or an *imagined* past event.

This is how we can achieve confidence and expertise by pretending to give a speech ahead of time in front of a mirror, before our appearance in front of a *real* audience. Our memory records this as a real, rather than an imagined experience. This is also why depression *feels* to be real life instead of a chemical imbalance accidentally set off. Below is an exercise where we "fight" stress symbolically.

Become-a-Matador Exercise

My daughter shared this excellent exercise with me. Imagine that your fears, self-recriminations, your "I'm-so-stupids" and "I'm-too-fats," your "I-can't-have-its" or "I-can't-do-its" are huge raging bulls snorting and charging at you. Name the bulls after each problem that is troubling you. Now imagine these terrible thought-and-image bulls charging at you, threatening great harm. When you see these thought-bulls coming at you, hold out your red matador's cape at arms length and simply let the bulls charge right by. Every time a thought-bull comes at you step aside as you hold out your arm with the red cape. Let them rage and snort *and go right on by you*! Try it right now. Close your eyes and envision one or two of your fears hurtling toward you, and then passing by.

The reason the mind can't distinguish between an imagined and a real event is that our memories are not held in a storage-and-retrieval system we can sift through like a mental Rolodex. Our memory is held more tentatively, *dispositionally.* There's always a slight difference in the firing of neurons.

Certain cells are *disposed* to register certain colors, sounds, etc. But in the absence of a specific stimulation, they can register something close to it; orange, for instance instead of pink. Experience shapes the changes of the memory circuits. The circuits are not just receptive to first experiences. They can be modified by later experiences throughout our entire lifetime. Our mind is quite malleable and thinks what we want it to think when we know how to work with it according to its nature.

Drawing a line in the sand of worry

It is human nature to worry and stew and fret about things. We all do it. But we don't have to do it to the point of becoming immobilized with self-focused and self-abusive thinking. Once we know how our brain works we can learn to stop our worrying *short* of triggering the fight-or-flight response that causes the "stress chemical dump."

We have to gird ourselves up and with the heart of a soldier make a firm stand, drawing a line in the sand of our worry and say, "This far I shall go and no more. I will not go *there*." You'd be surprised how many successful people, who've experienced seemingly insurmountable personal tragedies, actually say that very sentence to themselves. "I won't go there!" Then they don't! The way you don't go "there" is to go "somewhere else" in your mind. Your mind cannot follow two trains of thought going in different directions anymore than you can ride two trains going in two directions.

Is it hard to switch your train of thought when you are stressed? You bet it is. But it is doable. I have said something like this to myself during difficult times: "I can do this. I will gather my strength, I will do the best that I can. I will think about what I am doing. I will ignore my feelings."

The sympathetic mode (stressed) and the para-sympathetic mode (not stressed)

The fight-or-flight response is also called the *sympathetic mode* (named for the sympathetic nerves that are responsible for producing stress chemicals when the fight-or-flight response is triggered). The sympathetic mode is not an everyday state. It is a biochemical state of alarm. When our thoughts calm down, the alarm system turns off, the stress chemicals fade, and the body returns to the *para-sympathetic* mode. The *para-sympathetic* mode is our everyday state of okayness, wherein the body can rest and rejuvenate.

This is the reason stress causes illness. Only in the para-sympathetic (non-stress) mode does the body produce T cells necessary for a strong immune system. If we spend a lot of time with stressful thoughts our body will necessarily spend a long time in the sympathetic mode, and we will thus have a weak immune system.

Other problems from the fight-or-flight response

People who are depressed may also experience various other unpleasant physical symptoms such as: faster heart beat, sweaty hands, or shallow breathing. Your chest may feel painfully constricted. Your body may tremble, your head or hands may shake, your mouth may feel dry, your throat tight. You may have trouble swallowing or "catching your breath."

Sleeplessness and lack of appetite are well-recognized symptoms of depression. But you may also find you have been clenching your teeth or your fists for a long time without realizing it. If you take a minute out to relax your body you may find your "back is up," meaning that it is tight and tense.

Sometimes the heart beat is so fast, the chest so painful, and the breathing so constricted that people think they are having a heart attack. They are rushed to the hospital only to be told they are suffering from stress or even a full-fledged panic attack. Years ago this happened to me, at least twice.

All these anxiety symptoms are caused by the actions of involuntary nerves called sympathetic nerves (so called because they are "sympathetic" to anxious moods) as they release stress chemicals to various organs in the body as part of the fight-or-flight response.

We have no direct control over these sympathetic nervous reactions and cannot stop them *per se* when they start up. They follow the same pattern in every person. What's more, long after the original nervous thinking or stressful event has stopped, the chemicals still agitate around in our body causing these annoying, embarrassing, and painful symptoms—often culminating in depression.

We have *indirect* control over the triggering of the fight-or-flight response and subsequent production of stress chemicals in that we can change the stressful thinking that caused the sympathetic reaction in the first place. Then the symptoms will *subsequently* fade as the body ceases producing the stress chemicals. Anxiety will cease and depression will cycle down.

Is the battle really with depression?

Once we realize that depression is cyclical, we see that we have unlimited opportunities of getting out of it. It is cyclical remember, because it is part of our human psychological defense mechanism which isn't always turned on. Our defense system turns on and off depending upon how anxious our thoughts are. This includes thoughts we are aware of as well as thoughts of which we are not aware.

Our thoughts tell our brain when we're in immediate danger, real or imagined, and the defense mechanism triggers automatically. We can't stop it. We can't think stressful thoughts about how our boyfriend cheated on us and say, "Brain, listen up, I don't want you to prepare me for action so that I will get chemically imbalanced and feel stressed and then depressed. I just can't help thinking negative, anxious thoughts about that creep."

Too late! When the psychological defense mechanism is activated by stressful thinking, the fight-or-flight response gets us biochemically ready to do battle. Kill the tiger! Kill the boyfriend! Now, of course, we can't really kill our boyfriend. In the modern world it isn't always possible to take the immediate action our agitated defense instincts are calling for. So the battle is usually with ourselves.

But we don't *know* that. We *think* the battle is with our problems, or with our chemical imbalance, or our depression. In fact, the battle is with our own thinking. This is the reason we need to be more aware and observant of our thinking. We should not do our thinking behind our own closed doors. We need to drag our agitated thinking out into the light where we can see it, shake it out, and hang some of it on the line to dry while we calmly walk away from it!

Five

How Do We Think, Exactly?

If you don't know how you think, you won't understand how you get depressed.

In order to understand precisely how we think it is helpful to know the difference between thinking and feeling. Feelings and cognitive thinking originate in two entirely different parts of the brain. Most people use the terms "feeling" and "thinking" interchangeably, and it causes immense confusion in their lives. Our lives will not be tranquil as long as we continue to confuse our emotions with our reason.

For instance, "I feel you are wrong" is a thought not a feeling. "I feel like going to the movies" is also a thought. If it takes more than one word to describe it after you say "I feel," it is probably a thought. Feelings include: tired, angry, hurt, confused, happy, excited, peppy, uncomfortable, depressed, manic, hungry, thirsty, insulted. "I feel insulted" is a feeling but if you add "by you," then it becomes a stressful *thought* which provokes the *feeling* of anger.

The trouble with not recognizing the difference between thinking and feeling is that we often mistake our feelings for reality. This is the reason that when we're depressed we think our life is terrible when, in fact, we just *feel* terrible.

Mistaking feeling for thinking leads to dangerous over-concern and over-involvement with normal downer, negative, or anxious feelings. Because we don't understand exactly what causes these feelings, we give them too much importance instead of being able to ignore them by getting on with our regular daily activities. Paying attention to these feelings is the very thing that causes them to continue, and escalate, and assume tyrannical control over our lives. Paying attention to any thought or feeling is giving instructions to your brain that it is supposed to pay attention to them as well. Ignoring thoughts or feelings is instructions to your brain to ignore them.

Depressed patients often say they spend every moment fighting negative thoughts and feelings, without realizing that it is their very fighting that is the problem. In order to fight negative thoughts you have to keep thinking them, or they would not exist for you to have to fight them. The way to eliminate downer thoughts is not to fight them but to ignore them by thinking some other thought *instead* of the stressful one. This works for cancer patients. "I'm feeling better and better." It works equally well for depression. Thinking is very tricky. Once you learn the tricks you are the one in charge instead of your anxiety and depression.

The neurons of the brain

All our thinking and feeling is carried on by the neurons of our brain. Thoughts and feelings are both produced by the neurons. A typical brain is a system of some 100 billion cells—interconnecting neurons. The neurons communicate with each other by means of chemicals called neurotransmitters that receive, process, and transmit information through linked synapses. To loosely compare our thought process to a computer you could say that the neurons are "hardware" and our thoughts and feelings are "software." The hardware for cognitive and creative thought is located in the upper part of the brain, the neocortex. The hardware for feelings and emotion is in the lower part of the brain, the subcortex.

We are constantly changing the relationship between our thoughts and feelings. Unlike the computer, the brain is a living thing. When we change our software we also cause changes in our hardware. This is how we exchange new habits for old or learn new skills. Our behavior and thinking continually, throughout our entire lives, causes physical changes in the neurons of our brain.

To give you an idea of the brain's power let me cite a few facts from an article on brain structure by John Horgan in the October 2004 *Discover*: The brain is a thousand times faster than any known supercomputer. It is the most complex machine on the face of the earth. Synapses link each of our 100 billion cells to as many as 100,000 others. Hormones and neurotransmitters modulate the signals between the cells as these cell link-ups fade and strengthen according to experience.

The synapses in the brain can produce an astonishing quadrillion operations per second. Additional information computations may take place outside the synapses themselves. As the intensity of a stimulus increases, so does the firing rate of a neuron—200 peaks per second. Some neuroscientists think information may even be passed within the fluctuating gaps between the peaks themselves!

Many functions of the brain are autonomic and continue without our knowledge and without our need to intervene in their workings. The mind is not as fast as the brain. Our attention span can only accommodate one thought at a time. Therefore a great deal goes on in the brain of which the mind is unaware at any particular moment. These functions are generally referred to as "unconscious."

As complicated and rapid as the brain is, there is almost no function of it that we cannot influence by our own thinking or behavior. The use of hypnosis, instead of anesthesia, for major surgery is well known and documented. Many people have learned through imaginary visualization to mentally constrict the blood vessels in their brain, and send the extra blood flow into their hands. This alleviates the pain of migraine headaches which is caused by the engorgement of the blood vessels. Thousands have learned to "firewalk" over red-hot coals without burning the soles of their bare feet by concentrating on the thought "cool moss, cool moss."

How do we actually get from one thought to another?

The brain works by learned association (think "black" and the thought "white" will fire up; think "salt" and the thought "pepper" sparks up.) Any thought that is triggered in one neuron will cause similar, associated thoughts to spark up in other similar thought-related neurons, *like attracting like*, with increasingly wider participation by chance connections.

Learned associations determine your feelings and other biochemical responses, such as salivation, and the fight-or-flight response by the process of *classical conditioning*. You would not salivate at the thought "lemon" unless you had some prior experience (association) with its juicy, tart flavor.

We all have specific learned associations with particular thoughts, images, and words. These words and images, when thought, elicit chemical responses in our brains. These responses or feelings can't be changed directly by force of will. But they do fade as the thoughts which stimulated them cease to be thought, or as new thoughts are chosen in an effort to lessen the effect of a painful learned association.

The process of classical conditioning that causes learned association, is illustrated by that famous experiment of Pavlov and his dogs. The dogs were offered food and they salivated. Then for a period of time a bell was rung at the same time they were offered food. After a time the dogs salivated merely at the sound of the bell even when no food was offered. The dogs were "conditioned" to associate the thought of the bell with the thought of food which originally caused a biochemical response called salivation.

Learned association and depression

What does learned association have to do with depression? The next four paragraphs will explain the connection. Learned association facilitates a kind of networking of the brain through its memory banks. A neuron with a specific thought communicates it to another neuron with an associated thought memory, etc., forming a neural pattern or train of thought. If we could take a picture of the brain thinking some train of thought it would look like a streak of neuronal lightning, branching and forking across the sky of the brain as chains of individual neurons "talk" to each other through their synapses via their neurotransmitters.

The mind does not hear all this brain chatter. The mind hears only what it decides to "tune in on." And unlike tuning into some radio station, when we tune in to something going on in our brain, we immediately begin to influence it. Whatever *we* pay attention to, the *brain* pays attention to. This includes depression. When we change our thought and pay attention to something else, the brain changes and pays attention to something else.

The neuronal communication will change just because of our focus. For instance, if your boyfriend has caused hurt by cheating on you, one thought about him and your brain, *through learned associations between its neurons*, will immediately put you in touch with all the other errant boyfriends, betrayals, and disappointments in your neural memory banks with lightning speed. Thoughts are very quick, like the speed of electricity.

When we think the first depressed thought, it is learned association that causes the brain to get in touch with all the other similar downer thoughts we have lurking in the dark neuronal corners. As one negative thought sparks up another we get caught in escalating trains of anxious thought patterns. In this way we can get into a depressive neural pattern very quickly.

How acknowledging the pain of depression continues it

Remember, depression is caused by a chemical imbalance in the brain. This is very important because *there is a chemical consequence in the brain for every single thought we think.* So we want to avoid the kinds of thinking and learned associations that lead to the triggering of the fight-or-flight response that skews the chemical imbalance that leads to depression.

Once we are into depression, our attention is cemented in the subcortex and out of touch with the neocortex *except for* (and here is the important point) *the acknowledgment of the pain we feel.* This acknowledgment is the small bridge between the subcortex and the neocortex that becomes the conduit that allows depression to continue.

Depression continues because concentrating on the acknowledgment of the pain connects you (through learned association) with any other pain, stress, negative thoughts, anxiety, fear, etc., etc., in your memory banks. This causes the fight-or-flight response to continue to trigger, producing the stress chemicals that cause the subcortex to continue to produce more feelings of pain—a truly vicious cycle.

How you get out of depression instead of acknowledging it

Now here is the good news. Brainswitching can turn this small connecting conduit of acknowledging pain into the bridge that can *get you out of depression* instead of keeping you in it. How can this be accomplished? Again, by learned association.

The brain was built to be your most obedient servant. How do you command it? Since the brain works by learned association, whatever thought you think becomes immediately your specific instruction to the brain. The brain will rapidly pick up the thought like a football and start connecting it with all the other similar thoughts stored in its memory banks.

If you suddenly change and think a significantly different thought, the brain will change the direction of its previous train of thought and put you in touch with different stored memories similar to the new thought. Thus a new train of thought will begin to form.

When you think the first depressive thought, your obedient brain will scan its memory banks to connect you with any other thoughts similar to pain, fear, anxiety, or negative thoughts, etc., etc.

Brainswitching has you choose *a new thought which is a neutral or nonsense thought* that doesn't contain emotional associations. In effect, Brainswitching puts the very obedient brain into a mode of "treading water." The neutral thought will not be stimulating any anxious thoughts that trigger the fight-or-flight response. The chemicals will stop being produced, and the subcortex will stop producing pain, and stop sending pain messages up to the neocortex.

Learned association can get us into depression because some maverick thought can spark up and trigger old neuronal memories of the pain of depression. And learned association can get us out of depression through the process of Brainswitching. Learned association has the same effect on mania.

Mania

Mania is the other neuronal fork in the road to depression. You get to that fork the same way you get to depression, through anxious thinking that triggers the fight-or-flight response, causing stress chemicals to flood the body. If the series of learned associations lead to a mindset and pattern of behavior that has us withdrawing from everything and everybody, taking to our beds, and pulling the covers over our heads, we end up in depression.

The learned associations could, instead, lead to a mindset that moves us into some kind of *action*, rather than inaction. Thus we take the manic fork in the road. We may then latch onto some idea for an action or project that we obsess over, and inappropriately magnify. Then we could have what's known as mania. Action taken as a result of rational On-Purpose Thinking is different from mania. In mania the action is taken as a result of random thinking based on emotions.

Most people don't look for a cure for mania because it feels so good compared to depression. In fact, for some people mania is the *cure* for depression. But mania is the same as depression in its self-centered, self-focused thinking that is isolating from others, and therefore not centered in present reality. Sometimes, just by chance, manic ideas work. Most of the time they come to disaster.

Brainswitching is the alternative route out of depression and mania

We can *medicate* problem thoughts with antidepressants and we can also *change* problem thoughts as an act of will. This latter fact, which is the basis of Brainswitching, may be a new idea to you. By the time you finish the book, it will be second nature. Depression is terrifying because we know how easily we can fall into it. But it loses its power to frighten us when we also know a simple way *out*.

Remember that depression is cyclical. Once depression hits, it does not cease torturing us until some *random* non-depressive learned association pops up. Then the obedient brain turns away from the depressive pattern in a neuronal direction more compatible with the new thought. This random interruption of its thinking pattern by a maverick learned association causes more than depression to be cyclical.

Learned association, with its random interruptions, is also the reason the fight-or-flight response is cyclical, that it turns on and off. This would naturally be true because thoughts determine whether or not the fight-or-flight response is triggered, and learned association is the process we use to think.

There are many talented and creative people such as Beethoven, Van Gogh, author Henry James, and his brother, Dr. William James, "The Father of Psychology," who throughout their whole lives suffered frequent bouts of lengthy depression. They might have prevented their depression had they understood its cyclic nature.

They could have been forearmed had they realized the instinctive "fall-back" predilection of their own minds to revert to a defense mechanism, with the resultant negative, stressful, anxious thoughts that come with that defensive position. They could have used mental techniques to get out of it, once depression hit, if they had taken advantage of the pain receptor center in the neocortex. They would then have had the option to manage their moods by changing their thoughts before the fight-or-flight response was triggered that dumped the stress chemicals into their brains.

Learned association and neurotransmitters

The brain works by neurotransmitters such as serotonin. These are the biochemical reactions that allow the neurons to communicate. However, neurotransmitters are merely the chemical boats that carry the learned associations from one neuron to another. The neurons call for the boats when they are activated by a thought, so they can communicate it to another similar thought-related neuron. The brain is powered by thoughts in the same way that a car is powered by a motor. The brain is not powered by neurotransmitters. The neurotransmitters are more like the gas in a car.

How do we know thoughts power the brain?

Research shows that when an electron probe is touched to a living human brain it elicits a particular thought. When the probe is put to a different part of the brain a different thought is elicited.

We can make the brain work in the science laboratory by introducing electricity from the outside with an electron probe. Since we know there's no little electron probe that lives inside the brain, what generates the electricity in normal life?

The answer is that *thoughts* electrically power the brain. Brain scans show that when a person *thinks* a certain thought, neuronal activity lights up in a certain part of the brain, not in *all* parts of the brain. Some thoughts spark neuronal activity in the *subcortex*, the feeling part of the brain. Other kinds of thoughts spark neuronal activity in the *neocortex*, the thinking, cognitive part of the brain.

The brain works electro-chemically. Thoughts stimulate the neurons electrically, and then thoughts are communicated between the neurons chemically by neurotransmitters. Thoughts are what power the brain and rule the mind.

If a man sees a shadow on the ground and thinks "SNAKE," the thought will immediately stimulate a particular part of the brain and initiate a particular chain of thinking (through learned association) that will put him in a particular mind-set and cause the production of particular chemicals.

If he sees a shadow on the ground and thinks "ROPE," the thought will activate another part of the brain. If he looks at a *Playboy* centerfold and thinks "BABE," the thought will access yet another part of the brain and initiate another line of neuronal arcing that will put him in an entirely different mindset, with different chemicals produced.

Depression is also a mindset

We get to the depressive mindset the same way we get to any other mindset. We think our way into it. And just as we think our way *into* a mindset through learned association, we can also think our way *out* of it through learned association. One thought leads to another similar thought, etc., etc.

Again, this is the reason depression is cyclical. The mindset of depression can be temporarily interrupted by some maverick learned association that randomly sparks up. Or some outside circumstance might lead to alternative thoughts that can send the mind off in another direction away from depression. Remember, the brain always follows the direction of its most current dominant thought.

In the midst of a terrible depression you could win the lottery, or a fire could suddenly blaze up in front of you. The depressive thought pattern would then be interrupted by other kinds of thought leading the neural thought pattern away from the depressive mindset into another mindset. Like the mindset of buying a new car with your lottery winnings, or trying to save your life from a fire.

But we don't have to wait for circumstances around us to change so that our thinking can change. We can change our thinking anytime we want and interrupt the depressive mindset. We just have to remember that this is an option. This is the whole point of Brainswitching.

Six

Directed Thinking and Passive Thinking

The brain works all the time, with or without our awareness of its workings. There are two basic kinds of thinking all human beings do: Directed Thinking and passive thinking.

Last year on Spanish television I heard a story about this gentleman who knocks on his son's door. "Jaime," he says, "Wake up." Jaime answers, "I don't want to get up, Papa." The father shouts, "Get up! You have to go to school." Jaime says, "I don't want to go to school." "Why not?" asks the father. "Three reasons," says Jaime. "First, because it's so dull; second, the kids tease me; and third, I hate school." Then the father says, "Well, I am going to give you three reasons why you must go to school. First, because it is your duty; second, because you are forty-five years old, and third, because you are the headmaster." Wake up! Wake up! You've grown up. You're too big to be asleep. Wake up! Stop playing with your toys. (Anthony de Mello)

The brain is working all the time, with or without us, as far as our attention is concerned. All human beings do two basic kinds of thinking, Directed Thinking and passive thinking. Directed Thinking is when we are paying attention to our thinking. It is usually productive. It tends to be objective and more connected to the present reality of our everyday world. Brainswitching is a specific kind of Directed Thinking.

In Directed Thinking, also known as On-Purpose Thinking, we point the process of learned association in a particular direction, like getting dinner, writing a report, deciding to be cheerful, or making a cup of coffee. Our mind is focused into a pattern of thinking that helps us accomplish the task at hand. We reach for the coffee, then sugar or cream if we need it, etc., etc. Learned associations form a helpful mindset that directs our behavior.

Passive thinking

In passive thinking we have not, on purpose, set any particular line of thinking in motion. Our thoughts occur automatically and randomly progress along the lines of learned association as a matter of chance connections. In passive thinking the learned associations run amok, in any old direction: our ex-boyfriend's misdeeds, how we hate to get up and go to work, how nobody likes us, or how bad we feel. It is the mind at play with its toys (thoughts). Passive thinking *can* be productive, but it can also be very destructive.

The trouble comes when some maverick, anxious thought hooks up with a bunch of other like-minded fearful thoughts.

They spark each other into a thought pattern that directs our thinking down, down, down, triggering the fight-or-flight response, causing the production of stress chemicals and ultimately dumping us into depression.

As soon as we realize this is the muddy road where we're headed, we need to give our mind *alternate directions* to steer it back out of the mud. We should not let our thoughts wander around in some dark landfill of the mind and pitch us into despair. We should reach for Brainswitching.

What determines, precisely, which thoughts we think?

The choice of any particular thought is always ours, if we take it, by doing some kind of Directed Thinking or On-Purpose Thinking. Whether we choose a thought to think or not, the brain keeps on thinking anyway. The brain is always turned on even when we're sleeping. The neurons are always talking to each other. There is only a short while during the deepest sleep phase when the neurons do not communicate. If we don't choose a thought, sending our thinking in some specific direction, our thoughts will wander as they will in passive thinking.

Directed Thinking and passive thinking

The big difference between On-Purpose and passive thinking is that *passive thinking is automatic*. It comes unasked. It "pops up." It is instinctive. On-Purpose Thinking puts our brain to work for us at our express behest. It involves some intention and therefore some effort on our part. We must *intend* to think rational thoughts as an act of will to be sure to have them, for they will not *necessarily* appear on their own.

Passive thinking is the kind of thinking that leads to depression. Passive thinking is usually subjective, self-focused, and disengaged from people and things in our physical environment. Remember, when the brain/mind is left to its own devices, it is naturally inclined to go into its default mode. It reverts to its instinctive paranoid, looking-for-the-negative, defensive-guardian role.

We call passive thinking "letting the mind wander." When the mind wanders we can get into some terrible places. This is probably the basis of that old maxim, "An idle mind is the Devil's workshop," the "idle mind" referring to the fact that we are not actively directing it in some on-purpose, worthy pursuit.

Depending upon what kind of thinking you do, you can live your life subjectively or objectively. You can live your life by accident, or you can live on purpose. You can let your mind be molded by habitual, pop-up, maverick thoughts that lead you to be anxious and depressed due to the mind's guardianship default-mode. Or you can build the brain you want, one that is more calm, outer-directed, and connected to present reality because you have sent your thinking in that direction. Remember, when you exercise a thought, you make it dominant. The mind will go in the direction of its most current dominant thought.

Beware of passive, self-focused thinking

Since passive, self-focused thinking tends to disconnect you from others it can by itself be stress-producing. Consider the evolutionary principle, survival of the fittest. Obviously the "fittest" human being is the one who cooperates with and gets reciprocal support from others. We are herd animals who have evolved over the eons into the kind of creature that doesn't do well as a lone individual, adrift, outside of close society (as male pandas live for instance).

The more inwardly-focused and subjective our thinking is, the more we are separated from objective reality. If our consciousness has not been raised to *question* our own thinking, our physical and psychological isolation from our "regular world" may have us temporarily believing some real hogwash, and behaving in some very bizarre ways. This is the reason that *how we feel* cannot be our goal. *What we should do* must be our goal.

If we are unduly influenced by how we feel, we develop a turned-inward thinking that makes us overly vulnerable to the least bump in the road, and makes it hard for us to connect with others on a reciprocal give-and-take basis.

When we are disconnected physically, psychologically, or socially from our fellows, we get too self-focused. We feel vague, non-specific, and not-good feelings of strangeness and anxiety. This is the basic underpinning of that old syndrome variously and romantically described as feeling like "a stranger in a strange land." Our body experiences stress, our fight-or-flight response is awakened, and the delicate chemical balance of our brain begins to shift. We turn anxious.

Re-engagement helps us move out of self-focus

When we realize we are too self-focused we have to move forward, take a small step out and away from ourselves, even though we aren't sure of the way. People are always talking about the power of positive thinking. There is also the power of *positive doing.* In other words, you should never stay hunkered under the covers in bed when you are depressed. You need to do something physically and mentally active to start moving the learned associations in a more productive direction.

In the same way that depression alienates us, the smallest thing we do to pull ourselves out of depression usually hooks us right back up with others, either physically or symbolically. If nearest and dearest are close by when depression hits, reach out to them physically. Pat someone on the back, gently touch an elbow in passing, squeeze someone's hand, or give someone a momentary hug. Remember that you cannot touch someone without *being touched.*

You are *not* reaching out because you *feel* like reaching out. You are *not* reaching out because you *feel good.* You are reaching out because it is a good thing *to do* for yourself. Life is not a one-man show. An old saying is that "life is a relay race," and you can't run a relay race by yourself. Turning toward others helps us move away from our overly self-focused and subjective thinking. We begin to feel less anxious and alone with very small investments in other people.

In his book *The Instinct to Heal*, Dr. David Servan-Schreiber takes this idea even further.

> The idea that a loving relationship is *in itself* a physiological remedy, comparable to taking medication, rests on sound scientific ground—but it simply has not yet taken hold in the medical establishment.

Of course loving relationships take time and effort. Self-focus is easy. The passive thinking that leads to self-focus happens automatically, in the absence of Directed Thinking. Self-focus is also hard to move away from, especially when it has degenerated into depression. There is a reason we don't feel like doing anything else other than depression, and make no mistake about it, we *do* depression.

We do depression because we have a stronger genetic and more primal relationship to our own feelings than to the objective reality of our environment, even including the people we love. This is only too evident in spousal abuse. Feeling is automatic too, like passive thinking. Feeling is instinctive. It takes no effort to feel. It does, however, take effort to engage with our environment, with others. We have to will that. We do not have to will our feelings. They are self-triggering, automatic brain equipment.

One thought at a time

When we make that switch from self-focus to outward focus, since we can only think one thought at a time, we also loosen our focus on painful feelings. Anybody can do this momentarily with not much effort. Practice makes all the difference. As you practice switching focus from selfward to outward, you will get better and better at it. You will be able to maintain your chosen objective focus for longer and longer times until the chemical balance shifts back to normal.

I'm sure many of you would think that a decision to concentrate on the weave of sofa material is quite silly as a solution to depression. But try it when you are depressed, and you will see that as you concentrate on the material, really concentrate, your depression begins to recede. Have you ever seen those two-ways-to-see-it pictures that appear in old psych books? One picture looks at first just like a vase. But if you look again a slightly different way, it looks like two faces looking at each other. In another picture, if you look one way it is a picture of an old hag with a shawl, and if you look another way it is a pretty young woman.

You can quickly look back and forth at the picture from one aspect or the other, from one mindset to the other—old woman, young woman, old woman, young woman. But you can never see them both at once! That is because we can only think one thought at a time.

It is the same with depression and a decision to look at the sofa material. You will go back and forth from one mindset to the other, depression, sofa weave, depression, sofa weave. But you can't think both mindsets at the same time.

At this point I feel obligated to say that I find the Brainswitching word exercises are better than concentrating on the sofa weave. I only use the sofa weave for those early warning signs of depression, not the big hit.

Paradoxically, even the decision to try, as a mind trick, to make your depression worse will weaken it. You will be amazed that there is no way, as an act of will, to make your depression worse. This is because any on-purpose Directed Thinking trumps passive thinking. Any Directed Thinking fires up neuronal activity in the neocortex withdrawing energy from the subcortex. Even *trying to make your depression worse* is Directed Thinking, is On-Purpose Thinking, *not passive thinking.*

Seven

Where Is Depression Located in Our Brain?

When we know exactly what depression is, and where it is in our body, we don't feel so overwhelmed when it makes its appearance.

Winston Churchill referred to his chronic depression as the "Black Dog." Celebrity sufferers of depression and manic depression have variously described theirs as "The Noonday Demon," "The Edge of Darkness," "Darkness Visible," or "Touched With Fire."

If we don't know what depression is neuroscientifically we tend to supernaturalize it and horrible-ize it. We tend to see it as something extreme and terribly out of the ordinary. As separate from the regular workings of a normal brain. We mistakenly believe it is something uniquely visited upon us like some kind of psychological virus, some inherited mental abnormality, some overwhelming force, some brain illness. Something definitely "not us."

The worst thing is to think depression is *more powerful* than we are; to think it is something that can overwhelm us, can control us, terrorize us, inflict terrible pain upon us, force us to withdraw from regular life and pay attention only to it.

This self-denigrating delusion is caused by lack of more correct, practical information. It is further complicated by the superabundance of *misinformation* that tells us we are helpless in the face of depression, and there's nothing we can do about it except take drugs. There is a lot we can do about depression. As a matter of fact too many people, unknowingly, are already doing a lot to keep their depression going. We can also do a lot to stop it.

Depression is just a place in the brain

When you first realize that the mind is a defense mechanism, it may seem alarming. But as you become more and more familiar with the workings of the brain, the emotional ups and downs that used to be such a mystery will begin to make perfect sense. Not only that, you will find yourself more and more in control of those ups and downs. Awareness is half the battle.

Depression is a place in the brain we get to, the subcortex. By "get to" I mean that it is the place in the brain where all of our neuronal activity is arcing up. When we're depressed we have very little neuronal activity in the neocortex.

Depression happens only in the subcortex. There is never any depression in the neocortex. This is the reason we all notice the great schism between our cognitive faculties and our emotions when we are depressed. The important thing to remember is that this schism can be overcome by Brainswitching and Directed Thinking.

When we're depressed we find that we have great difficulty concentrating on anything. But wait! We fail to realize that we are already concentrating extremely well—on our depression going on in the subcortex. This is the reason we don't have much brain activity happening up there in the neocortex! We can learn to switch our concentration, even in the midst of a deep depression, from being depressed to *getting out of depression!*

When we have depression going on in the subcortex we need not stay there, neuronally speaking. By "stay there" I mean we need not continue to focus our attention on the subcortex. It is very seductive but nothing is *forcing* us to concentrate on our depression. Instead, we can think specific thoughts which re-situate our neuronal activity in the neocortex. Then from the area of the neocortex we can fool our brain into becoming calm and to stop producing stress chemicals.

We can always escape the depression going on in the subcortex by taking temporary refuge in the neocortex where there is no depression. We do this by using simple Brainswitching exercises similar to the first two you have already seen. Remember, certain thoughts stimulate neural activity in the subcortex and other thoughts stimulate neural activity in the neocortex.

How do we know that there is no depression in the neocortex?

Neuroscience has documented this by brain-mapping the neuronal and behavioral activity of people who have survived accidents that left them with significant brain tissue damage.

People who have no damage in the area of the neocortex, but have sustained significant tissue damage in the subcortex can completely lose the faculty of producing *any* emotion. These people retain all their cognitive faculties. They know all that they knew before the damage occurred. They can still do complicated crossword puzzles or higher math. But they are incapable of feeling any emotion. These people can remember and tell a joke, but have lost the capacity to think it is funny. And they *cannot* suffer depression.

This scientific finding was probably what led to the tragic pre-frontal lobotomies in the 1950's where this critical part of the emotional brain was surgically removed from the severely depressed patient. Now, of course, we know that people need their emotions for decision making, and cannot function in the world and live independently without them.

A startling neuroscientific fact about feeling

Now here's the truly remarkable neuroscientific finding that I have never seen mentioned in all the psychiatric literature about depression. It is one of the most important reasons that Brainswitching works for depression.

We all feel our emotions very deeply and the effect of the environment upon us. But in order to feel *any* emotion, or the pain of some bodily injury (which are all produced in the subcortex) we must make a cognitive *judgment* in the neocortex about the thing we are feeling! Signals from the nerve endings in our arm if we cut our skin, or signals from the subcortex that emotion is going on must move upward to the neocortex and be received and acknowledged there before we can feel them!

Cases have been recorded of athletes who actually break a bone during the heat of a game and don't experience any pain until after the competition is over. Their neocortical thought concentration on the game blocked the pain signals being sent to the neocortex that should have alerted them to the pain of their injury.

We must make a judgment about pain before we can feel it? Does this sound like a theory? It isn't. It is a neuroscientific fact also proved by neuro-imaging people who have experienced brain damage in the neocortex.

Some people have no damage in the subcortex but have sustained severe damage in the neocortex in the place that *receives* the signals from the subcortex. These people, with neocortical damage, will not be able to feel or experience the emotion or pain they produce in the subcortex anymore than those aforementioned victims of subcortical damage who can't produce the subcortical feelings in the first place.

We control our feelings by controlling our thinking

The other proof of the fact that we must acknowledge our feelings in the neocortex before we can feel them is this: hypnosis *can substitute for general anesthetic* in major surgery. People do not feel pain when their neocortex is convinced (hypnotized) that pain is not happening, even though their flesh is being cut by the surgeon's knife and impacting the subcortex.

You don't have to remember all of this information about judging feelings in the neocortex. What it means, practically speaking for depression, *is that we can manage our pain and emotion in the subcortex by controlling our thinking in the neocortex.*

This is nothing new. Successful people have always lived their lives by reason rather than emotion. However, this kind of mind-management has not been applied specifically and forcefully to depression as it should be.

The medical profession has come around in *other* areas. Doctors are curing ADD and Irritable Bowel Syndrome with hypnosis and guided imagery. (Sandra Blakeslee, "Hypnosis Gains Respect, Helps to see Brain Work," *The New York Times*, November 23, 2005).

It is important to mention here that in the organization of the nerve cells that carry sensory information, there are *ten times* more nerve fibers carrying information from the top down than from the bottom up; from the neocortex to the subcortex rather than the other way around. This indicates the amount of power available to us to get the cognitive part of our brain, once we learn how to access it, to manage the emotional part.

When we earnestly apply this top-down idea to depression, we can see that it is possible to make the personal decision that self-abusive thinking, such as the anxious worry that leads to depression, is simply no longer an option for us. Whenever we notice this painful thinking occurring to us, we can immediately choose specific thoughts which stimulate the neurons in the neocortex. This will draw neuronal energy from the subcortex and then the painful emotions in the subcortex slowly power down. It also accomplishes "thought-jamming" of problem thoughts so they don't continue.

Freedom of the Will

Our thinking determines our emotions. As our thinking moves to anxious, our feelings become anxious. As our thinking changes out of anxious and moves to calm, our feelings change from anxious and move to calm. Our *minds* know we are in charge of our feelings, even if *we* don't.

Because thoughts trump feelings, reason always trumps emotion. The top-down sensory information channels of the brain are set up that way. But for any trump card to win *you have to play it.* We have to learn how to call upon our reason, how to call upon our neocortex when our emotions have us distracted with the agony of all that painful feeling going on in the subcortex.

By the way, this is the neuroscientific explanation for the ancient concept Freedom of the Will: We are not forced to function from instinct, we may choose to function from reason. How a person manages to make this choice, neurologically speaking, is to choose particular thoughts that will spark neuronal activity in the particular part of the brain from where they wish to function: the intellect of the neocortex or the emotions of the subcortex.

We always have the choice of which part of our mind to use–the subcortex or the neocortex. This is also the neuroscientific explanation for Spinoza's claim that *"Will and intellect are one and the same thing."*

Eight

Brainswitching in a Nutshell: Why Some People Don't Get Depressed

Biology is not destiny; will is destiny.

Remember, the mind does whatever thinking you instruct it to do. You tell it what kind of thinking to do by the particular thought you are thinking. If you want your mind to do depression, start thinking a depressive thought. If you want your mind to do happy, think a happy thought.

Here's where magical thinking comes in handy. The brain doesn't know the difference between being happy and *pretending* to be happy. Happy thoughts ultimately stimulate happy feelings. The feelings are genuine even if the thoughts that encouraged the production of those feelings were fake. This is the reason that groups of people all over the country meet regularly every morning for 30 minutes of laughing out loud.

In the next four paragraphs I will describe to you exactly what Brainswitching is. However, you may still need the supporting information and evidence in the subsequent chapters to fully understand and take advantage of it.

Brainswitching is a psychotherapeutic technique that came from neuroscience research and hypnosis. It handles stress, anxiety, and depression from the "feelings receptor station;" a specific small area in the neocortex. This is the part of the neocortex that requires us to make a judgment about what we are feeling in order to be able to feel it.

Brainswitching is different from psychotherapy

Most other psychotherapies, or stress management methods, focus on the subcortex: by zapping or eradicating feelings temporarily with electro-shock; by deadening them with drugs; or by trying to alter negative thinking with talk therapy.

Brainswitching does not work directly on the feelings themselves, or even on the thinking that produced the feelings in the first place. It works on this neuroscientific fact: Although all our feelings are produced in the subcortex, we can't actually feel our feelings unless messages about their occurrence in the subcortex are duly received and acknowledged in the neocortex. Simple exercises indirectly manage subcortical feelings by using repetitive, thought-jamming words, phrases, or even nursery rhymes to distract this small area of the neocortex *whose sole duty is to acknowledge and judge feelings so that we can feel them.*

What if the mind dredged up a habitual depression or anxiety attack for me and I didn't want to go there? Brainswitching is the answer to this question. Simple exercises and "thought-jamming" mind tricks such as saying repetitively "green frog, green frog," or some nursery rhyme, or "yes, yes, yes" distract the cognitive focus on feelings at the site of the neocortex. The stressful feelings of depression and pain *can't be thought* because they are repetitively being replaced by non-stressful thoughts. Since the stressful thought is side-lined, the fight-or-flight response ceases to be triggered and the chemical balance normalizes.

We all get depressed

It is generally believed that *some* people get depressed and *other* people don't. Since depression is part and parcel of our psychological defense system, the fact is that *everybody* gets depressed. Those who get out of depression quickly, however, usually describe themselves also as "people who don't get depressed."

They don't get depressed because they have learned mind techniques, probably picked up as children, that allow them to disengage from stressful thinking *before* their fight-or-flight response triggers. Remember, it is the release of fight-or-flight stress chemicals that causes the chemical imbalance that leads to depression.

People who claim they never get depressed already know how to brainswitch, though they might not be aware of it. If you don't naturally get yourself out of depression this way, fear not. You can learn how to do it. Some people already know the difference between passive and On-Purpose Thinking, even though they may not label their thinking with these terms. When you have an intellectual grasp of the different kinds of thinking available to you, you will be able to make more proactive choices during times of emotional turmoil. You will have more options than just the usual roller coaster ride on your feelings.

All brains are not the same

The thinking habits of people who easily get out of depression are different from people who haven't learned those techniques. People who get out of depression also react much differently to the first warning signs of depression. There is a reason for this.

The brains of people who can get out of depression are different from those who can't. This, also, need not be a problem for those who are depressed. The thinking exercises in this book can change your brain. They can literally build neuronal pathways that you can take right out of depression.

Sounds impossible? It isn't. It is just basic biology. Human brains may all look pretty much alike, sitting side by side in laboratory jars. But real, live brains are very different from one another. They're different because our brains are constantly being re-constructed and re-ordered according to how we *use* them.

Thinking and behavior continually shape our brain physiology. New thought patterns, new neuronal pathways are day-by-day, action-by-action, neuron-by-neuron, being built out of our current daily experience. If this were not so, we could not learn a new word, much less develop a skill like figure skating or playing the piano. Neither could we form a new habit, good or bad. Neither could we learn how to get out of depression when it hits.

Different people have different reactions when hit by depression

One reaction to the onset of depression is to succumb to one's emotions. As you do this habitually, the symptoms can get out of hand. In some ways depression is the ultimate "mission creep" as the behavior escalates to accommodate the feelings. What starts out as being non-talkative and non-responsive can turn into full-fledged catatonia, a withdrawal into complete non-communicativeness.

Another reaction to the onset of depression is to quickly do some mental exercise or thought-jamming mind tricks that keep you from thinking about how bad you feel. One of the habits that depressed people have is withdrawing from regular life, disengaging from their normal routine, collapsing into depression, and following rote syndromes of reactive behavior and learned helplessness.

These syndromes don't *seem* like choices to people who suffer from them. But to those who clearly know the difference between passive thinking and Directed Thinking, these depressive symptoms *will be* seen as choices. If you are not yet a person who can see which depressive symptoms are choices, and which are not, don't worry. This book will show you exactly what they are.

Do not be concerned if you did not acquire, as a child, the particular bit of emotional intelligence that allows you to avoid depression. You can learn it as an adult. Depression does not necessarily mean that you have a mental illness. It may simply mean that you do not yet have the necessary information to "take care of business" when depression hits. Reading this book is giving you that information right now.

Since I am one of those adults myself who learned on my own how to get out of depression, believe me I understand any skepticism you may have at this point. Not only did I have to learn the techniques, I had to create them, quite awkwardly at first. But after a year or two I had perfected a Brainswitching and thought-jamming process that is wonderfully successful for me and thousands of other formerly depressed people.

Anybody can learn how to get out of depression

At one time I thought I had to meekly submit to any depression that came down upon me. Likewise I thought that some people, like my husband, were immune to depression, lucky them. After one of my lectures my husband told me he had once thought so too, "But listening to your explanation about

Brainswitching exercises changed my mind. I remembered that, from the time I was a young boy, whenever I felt myself feeling really low and despairing I would immediately imagine some great football or baseball game that I had seen. I would go over and over some favorite play in my mind and I would be the one carrying the ball."

The reason my husband never got depressed is that as a child he built in his brain a small but important neuronal connection from his depression to his rational thinking. He continued to use this connection for the rest of his life. Later, he used other distractions than football plays. In this way he would escape from his agitated subcortex and take refuge in his neocortex whenever depression hit.

Others have told me similar stories. Several said that they never got depressed "like some people I know" because whenever they started to feel bad, they would distract themselves by singing songs, or repeating some favorite poem like the 23rd Psalm.

One woman said she often visited her aunt who lived a hard life on an isolated farm. She remembered the many times she would find her aunt at work in the kitchen just singing for hours. "My aunt knew these old country ballads, and each of them must have had 30 verses. I'm sure that's how she kept herself from being depressed." The woman is correct, and there is a good neuroscientific reason for it. Singing sparks up neuronal activity in the neocortex, withdrawing energy from the subcortex.

Singing a song can get you out of depression? You must be kidding!

At this point I would not be surprised if you didn't see how singing a nursery rhyme could get you out of depression. Singing a song is such a simple thing to do. What is complicated is to give you the interconnecting, neuroscientific reasons that it works so that you will do it, instead of dismissing it as simplistic.

Sing-a-song type solutions are not as easy as they seem. It is hard to learn things as adults that children pick up so easily. Children don't question the whys and wherefores; it's monkey see, monkey do. That is one of the reasons they suggest violin lessons at the age of 3.

We adults must do things the hard way. We have to figure it all out *intellectually* first before we're willing to go forward. Another problem is that psychoanalysis dominated psychiatry in the 1950s. Our whole culture has been taught an undue reverence for feelings, and undue fear of the compulsive thinking and behavior that our feelings bring us to.

The next chapter tells about my first clumsy experience with Directed Thinking, and how I stumbled across the idea that such a thing as Brainswitching could work. The importance of this story is that my very first bumbling attempt worked at all! It should give you some confidence that even your first stab at Brainswitching will be of some help right away, and it is something that improves greatly with practice.

Brainswitching works

Here's a note I received recently from someone who had severe depression for many years: "The techniques you teach work most of the time and I've kept myself alive this whole year as a result of using these techniques. I hold down a steady job, I'm never late and I never miss a day. I'm able to live on my own, have friends, take care of myself, and pay bills etc."

Here's another: "Becoming aware of the 'depressing' thoughts is the major hurdle. My mantra lately, when a negative thought (about anything really) hits, is 'BEGONE!' (caps intended). This has helped me immensely, even if it means saying it over and over and over again. My days of depression are fewer and far between. Being aware forces me to choose, act, and do something about the situation, or choose to stay put in the situation, but then stop whining."

And another: "I've been so much better since I first read your book a couple of years ago. The black cloud of depression comes along and now I choose to run out from under it. Sometimes it takes me a while longer to realize I'm under it than other times. But I'm learning to recognize the signs and get busy with other thoughts and actions."

This excerpted review was posted on amazon.com

I don't always hear directly from people who have used my methods. Sometimes I hear about them indirectly. Of course this following review is personally rewarding to me (you can read the complete review for yourself on amazon. com) but I include it, with the author's permission, for other reasons than just patting myself on the back. It might be very comforting to know that a woman could be in such a desperate situation, as you or your loved one might be in, and was able to overcome it, by herself, without drugs.

> I wrote my first review of this book in November, 2001, but I wanted to follow up, and since I can only have one review on here, I am consolidating {them}... It has now been more than three years since I read DEPRESSION IS A CHOICE, and I am cured of my depression. It is no longer a factor in my life. This book gave me the tools that I needed, and after awhile, I didn't even need to employ them actively anymore. It became a natural way of being. Once in awhile, I do wake up with a hint of depression, but it is rare, and I make it go away easily. I have also learned to coexist with feelings that can be painful, depending on life circumstances, but not give into them. I am NOT my depression. My depression is only a feeling, and it can no longer stop me. I learned this because of this life-saving, amazing book. Best wishes in your journey to feeling better. It is definitely possible.

This is the woman's original review: three years earlier:

> I put myself into a psychiatric hospital when I was 20. I was there for three months before they would release me. I have suffered deep depression for the last twelve years, since that

time, and prior to that, for as long as I could remember, although not as severe. I am now 32. I can't hold onto a job, because every time I have to work I am miserable, and I fall apart. Most days, I can't do much at all. My family tries to tell me I need medicine, as have doctors in the past. I tried that a couple of times when I was younger, but I have always known that can't be the only answer. Therapy was never-ending…I was never sure that I would ever get past it and be able to live a more 'normal' life. Then I stumbled upon this book.

DEPRESSION IS A CHOICE is a book with guidelines for people like me. I have only known one way of acting. Of feeling the chemical and emotional pain and giving into it. That it wasn't my fault, but I had to ride it out, and that depression would come whenever it wanted, and sometimes when things were going great, out of nowhere.

This book taught me some practical steps I can take to intervene when the pain starts to set in. It takes some effort, but it is doable. Since beginning this book, I have found that sometimes I would rather be depressed than to direct my thought. Sometimes my depression is comforting; familiar. Other than the torture, hopelessness, and helplessness that it brings when it arrives, it doesn't require me to do anything but to suffer. Now that I know it is even POSSIBLE, I will choose not to let depression take over me, while sometimes still feeling the pain of it. I have had the need to use this every single day since I started reading the book, since I feel depressed at least once a day, and it has worked for me!

I can understand that people who have suffered like I have may be angry at this book. It is painful to realize that

what we have learned in therapy and incorporated as a belief
system, which feels so right, could possibly be wrong (that
we are victims, and that there are limited solutions, if any, to
dealing with our mental illnesses). I started to believe that I
would, for the rest of my life, be the victim of my depression
whenever it tried to take over. After reading this book, I
know better now… Thank you Ms. Curtiss! You have saved
my life as I have known it for too long.

We can control only what we are aware of and we can learn
to be more aware. We do not have to live habitual lives with
the automatic thoughts, re-played emotions, and mechanical
reactions that cause chemical imbalance. We can learn how
our brain works.

Taking your mind away from depression

Putting a stop to your depression is no more technically
difficult than learning how to stop a car. But we are *forced* to
learn how to operate a car in order to get a license, and nobody
has ever forced us to learn how to operate our own mind.
Until we know how it works, we tend to be the *passenger* of
our mind instead of the *driver*. We need a better operation
manual than a bunch of platitudes like "think positive," or
"be grateful," or "snap out of it," or "raise yourself up by your
own bootstraps." We need *operating instructions*.

Once we understand the operating instructions then, only,
do the platitudes start to make sense. Why shouldn't we learn
how to operate our own mind? We wouldn't dream of driving
a car without knowing how to control such a complex and

powerful machine. We learn how to start and turn off the engine. We learn where the gas and brake pedals are, study the basic traffic laws, and get some driving practice on empty side streets before we take on the Expressway. But most of us *haven't the slightest idea where are the brakes and gas pedals to our own mind.* We don't know how to stop at our own emotional red lights.

Chronic anxiety and depression are *not necessary.* Our brain is only one part of us. We, the totality, are more powerful then the pharmaceutical industry would have us believe. We are more powerful than our feelings. Feelings are data, *not imperatives.* Letting feelings direct our lives is like starting our car, releasing the brake, stepping on the gas, and *refusing to steer.* MINDCRASH! We can do better.

When we realize lower brain feelings are running our lives, we need to "take the car keys away" by Brainswitching. This will get us back up into the reasoning power of the neocortex, where there is no anxiety or depression. But we need to understand *where* our power lies in order to *use* it.

Nine

Desperation Is the Mother of Brainswitching

Chance favors the prepared mind.
— Louis Pasteur

The pain of depression cannot think itself; *we* must think it. The mind is like a CD player where thoughts are the CDs. Our CD player can only play one CD at a time. While one CD is playing, such as the depressive thought "I am depressed," all other CDs must wait their turn. If we don't want the mind's painful-thought CD, we can decide to put in another. The pain may echo in us as a physical feeling for a short while. But if we insist on putting our preferred-thought CD back each time our mind, out of habit, rejects it, the preferred one will soon "stick." Then the depressive CD will stay "off-line." The stress chemicals that were caused by the fearful CDs will begin to fade and our pain will disappear.

We can change our painful and negative moods indirectly by choosing neutral or nonsense thoughts that shift our attention from the subcortex to the neocortex which, as we have learned, does not contain stress or depression. This is the basis of Brainswitching. I'm a psychotherapist, but there are a lot of psychotherapists around. How did I come to think of it?

I like to compare Brainswitching to the paper clip. This practical item wasn't in use until the 20th Century when Johan Vaaler received an American patent for his invention in 1901. It's such a good idea, what took so long? At first people used thread to sew important papers together. Then the straight pin was invented in 1835, and was used as a kind of pre-staple. John Vaaler was a scientist, but there were a lot of scientists around. How did he come to think of it? I can just imagine him fiddling around with a piece of wire and paper. Suddenly, there it is! Once made, of course, the paper clip looks so self-evident that anybody at all could have done it simply by chance.

The following incident was the very ignominious beginning of my first bumbling attempt at Brainswitching. Of course I didn't call it that at the time. The name came much later. That day I wasn't trying to invent a system. I was trying to save my life.

I was very unhappy

In those days I was often depressed, full of panic and anxious worry that would last for days, or months at a time. I would plug along in my dull gray world, hugging my children with wooden arms, eating food that tasted like cardboard. My heart was usually stuck halfway up into my throat, and tense, fitful sleep produced little rest.

I can remember wondering if I would ever be happy like other people. I never felt safe from the instant agony that could engulf me anytime it wanted. Even on good days I feared that depression was always hanging just nearby. For people with severe depression life is like walking on a thin crust, and just below Hell is waiting, waiting for the moment when you can no longer hang on to the ground of your life.

Of course I could have hung onto my life then, but I didn't yet know how to do it. I was a sitting duck for the first wave of depression. It would be like the sky turned suddenly black and I'm transported to a lonely frozen lake. I hear the sickening crack of the ice, and I'm far from shore. And now I know I'm going to fall in and be lost, lost.

Panic attacks too

Sometimes depression would implode into a full blown panic attack. My throat would close. It was hard to breathe or swallow. My heart would start racing and pounding. Twice my husband rushed me to the hospital, convinced it was a heart attack. All this time, I was buying mind-power and self-help books that basically told me my problem was that I didn't "think positive."

One day I thought I couldn't hang on any longer. I was not going to make it. I knew I needed help and called my psychiatrist. Except for my scheduled appointment later in the week, there were no openings. My husband was at an all-day meeting. I felt abject terror. I need help, I thought

"TODAY, NOW, IMMEDIATELY!!! Oh God, Somebody has to help me."

At this point I was crawling on the floor, writhing in agony, weeping, rolling myself over and over, back and forth, back and forth, banging myself up against the wall. The pain was excruciating. I thought I would do ANYTHING to get relief. I was willing even to try one of the stupid suggestions from those books and think some positive thought. But thrashing around in my pitiful, groveling mind, I couldn't come up with any positive thought.

Drowning in my pain and desperation, the best I could do was "green frog." I wasn't sure that "green frog" was a positive thought. But it didn't seem like it could possibly be a negative one. Besides, it was the only thought that came to me in my extremis. I clung to it for dear life.

Brainswitching was born

Every time another tidal wave of depression began to drown me, I grabbed onto that thought like a life preserver. "GREEN FROG. GREEN FROG. GREEN FROG." I didn't say it gently. I SCREAMED it in my mind, "GREEN FROG. DAMMIT ALL TO HELL. GREEN FROG."

Like a dog with a bone, I held on. After twenty minutes or so of hanging on to "green frog" I "came to the surface a little." The desperation of pain and panic seemed to have faded. I could breathe okay. I didn't feel real great, but not real terrible either. I felt tired, tentative, and wary, like the uneasy relief after your headache's just barely gone, and you're scared it might come back any second. My depression seemed lifted. I wasn't sure it was really gone, but I wasn't going to look around for it either. Wasn't sure if "green frog" had had anything to do with anything.

Maybe it worked

I "got into it" really bad a couple of days later, and again grabbed for "green frog" like a kind of "rabbit's foot." *Who the heck knows if it really helps.*

Again, I felt better in about twenty minutes. In time I got better and better at substituting "green frog" for whatever painful feelings or anxious thoughts were bothering me. There is no particular magic to "green frog," as I found by experimenting with other nonsense phrases. I got depressed often enough to try out any number of them. They all worked. It's not the content, it's not the particular word of the Brainswitching exercise that's important, it's the process itself.

Repetition is the key

I don't even need to know, specifically, which stressful thoughts I'm replacing. If I think neutral thoughts for a time, the depression *always* goes away, no matter what thoughts caused it in the first place. The power of Brainswitching is not the greatness of the thought. The power is in the consistent, repetitive, conscious choice of *your thought* over your mind's autonomic depressive thought.

There's a distinction between Brainswitching and regular cognitive behavior therapy. The repetitive choice of a simple neutral or nonsense phrase, over and over, can cause a self-hypnotic trance that can reach deep into the mind's autonomic processes to alleviate the symptoms of depression in the subcortex by distracting our neocortical acknowledgment of it.

It works for her!

A woman posted on her Internet blog the following comment about the "green frog" exercise: "My husband said, 'Don't just sit around being depressed, fix it!' So I went out…and got two books: Depression is a Choice and The Depression Workbook. The workbook is such a piece of s***. 'How do you feeeeeeeel?' 'Whyyyyy do you think you feeeeeeel that way?' 'What's the earliest point you remember feeeeeling that wayyyyy?' 'What can other people do to make you feeeeeel better?' THEY CAN STOP ASKING ME ABOUT MY FEELINGS!!!! Holy cow. If I wanted to think about my feelings, my husband wouldn't be saying 'You need to tell me about your feelings.' I sure as s*** don't want to sit down and wallow in the damn things. On paper!

"I much, much prefer the other book, even though it p****s me off… the damn woman goes on and on and on about the same flipping thing for hundreds of pages. OK! I GOT THE POINT THE FIRST TIME YOU SAID IT! Jeezy chreezy. Also, blame the victim much? But, dammit, she's totally right. It's a choice to be depressed. Just because I feel depressed doesn't mean I have to pay attention to it, and I totally can distract myself from it. (See what I mean? Annoying, isn't it? I'd be REALLY mad if it didn't work). I'm totally NOT DEPRESSED right now, and it's because (at this woman's suggestion) I sing 'Frere Jacques' (the singing was her idea, that was just the first song I thought of) to myself in my head, really loud, whenever I feel it coming on, and that distracts me to where I start thinking about something else. When I don't want to get out of bed, I just get the f*** out of bed and get the f*** on with my life. Eventually I quit whining to myself."

An amazon. com review about the exercises:

...That's when Curtiss' technique of "Directed Thinking" saves the day. I can get myself out of the depressed mood by choosing different thoughts which then change my mood. That's all depression is, after all–a temporary mood that engulfs me because of some thoughts that I'm generating. I am free to direct my thoughts the same way I direct my cursor to tell my computer what I want it to do.

Depression needs to be understood and by-passed, not cured

Patients often say that they want to get rid of these terrible thoughts and painful feelings. They want to get them *out of their heads*. The best news in the world is that you don't have to get rid of anything. You will always carry around in your head, somewhere in your memory banks, every terrifying, frightening thought you've ever had; every horror movie you've watched; every agonizing feeling you've ever felt. However, you are never compelled to revisit any of them. You decide what thoughts should recede back into the far tomb of thought archives by refusing to entertain them for more than a nanosecond when they pop up. When you don't entertain them, after a while they stop popping up. You never have "to go there." They cannot interrupt your life without your express permission. They can't "cause" you to do anything.

Our symptoms are not caused by depression

This may be a hard concept at first. But soon you will begin to see that you have been *misled* into believing that the things you do when you get depressed are *caused* by your depression: the heavy sighs, the sad face, the slowed movements. In reality, depression does not *cause* any behaviors and *it doesn't need to be cured*. Depression is part of our psychological defense mechanism. Depression simply needs to be understood, acknowledged, and ultimately ignored once it has been neutralized by mind tricks.

It is immensely helpful to remember that we never have to *behave* like we're depressed. We can always choose which behaviors we wish to engage in whether we're horribly depressed or not. Just because we have always behaved a particular way—crying, going to bed, not engaging in regular activities, withdrawing from people, believing ourselves to be helpless, thinking how life is pointless— doesn't mean that we have to keep doing that. Remember, thinking is also behavior. A thought is just a thought, but thinking is behavior. Just because we have always done things one way doesn't mean we can't choose to do them another. *Our behavior immediately following a depression hit determines how long it will last.*

You need a plan

Intellectual understanding alone is not enough when depression whams you upside the head. You need a plan ahead of time. You need to know exactly, specifically, what mind exercise, what specific poem or nonsense phrase you are going to use. Once depression hits, it's too hard to think any other thought other than the thought that you are depressed. You need to have a substitute thought for the depressed thought "at the ready" that you have decided to use no matter how you feel.

Prepare two or three different exercises such as a nursery rhyme, some phrase like "green frog," or some dumb song that is easy to sing repetitively. Start with one, and if it doesn't feel like it is working right at that moment, quickly choose another. Then hunker down with your chosen phrase or song, and hang on to it. Keep choosing it again when you lose concentration.

Remember that thoughts are very quick, so you don't have to worry that any depressive thought is going to overwhelm you. A depressive thought is over as quick as any other. It's just that you have feared depression for so long. Fear is very painful until you accept it and move ahead. How do you accept pain? You say okay and relax into it as you think about it. You will get much better at this in a very short time. As soon as the edge is off the major pain, get going on morning exercises or chores, and ease into your regular schedule. Don't forget to concentrate on what you are *doing*, not what you are *feeling*.

Don't let depression fool you

You might think you can't get rid of depression when you have real things to be depressed about. But depression is not real life. Depression is a panic room of the mind. We always want to get back out of our panic room into real life again, and then we will be better able to handle our problems.

Depression is a chemical state of alarm that we have somehow built into a holding room. Once the alarm goes off we are not supposed to suffer from the alarm itself, or even worse take up residence in it. We are supposed to move into action that the alarm has roused us to. Or, if the alarm goes off, and we realize there is no problem, we have to turn off the alarm so it doesn't continue to agitate us.

We can always lessen our depression by exercise, or physically getting to work on some problem. But if this is not practical, mental exercises and mind tricks will do. By working on a problem symbolically we also accomplish something very important. The mind will be satisfied and calmed that *something is being done.*

A real event would be physically jogging. An imagined event would be doing imaginary jogging. Both would have a calming effect on the mind. As we have learned already, the mind, in retrospect, cannot tell the difference between an imaginary event and a real one. That's also the reason our fears, our imaginings, and our depression turn into our reality.

Move ahead with the "new normal"

Once our mind tricks set us in the direction away from anxiety and depression, we can move to more productive action. Although some might think that any action that gets them out of the agony of depression is, ipso facto, productive.

When the situation has quieted down and becomes the "new normal," we can do some self-inquiry work to gird ourselves for the next flare-up. We could, for instance, think about something like the precept of Marcus Aurelius: "At any moment I will cling to nothing else, save reason alone." Then, when the next emotional trauma hits, we can grab onto this to remind ourselves that we should not forget to use our rational faculties to calm our emotional upsets.

Marcus Aurelius' phrase is not just an empty platitude. In thinking about it we are building a neuronal link, by the process of learned association, from the emotional limbic system to the reasoning faculties of the neocortex. Then when emotional trauma hits, we have a small but important neuronal connection to our rational thinking.

The biggest complaint of people who come in for psychotherapy for depression is that they seem to loose all connection to their reasoning faculties. They can't concentrate, can't read, are unable to think clearly about anything. We can build those connections to our cognitive faculties with thoughts—-the same way we would build a bridge with cables.

I, myself, often think about that Marcus Aurelius phrase so that it becomes a strong enough neuronal link that it will show up when I need it. I have also programmed into my neural network the phrase "I am not my pain, I am the observer of my pain, and I must identify with the observer rather than the pain." The observer of course, being the part of you that is not the emotional part. The observer would be the rational part of you.

When can I finally just be happy?

I get quite a few letters from people that use Brainswitching and Directed Thinking to get out of painful depressive episodes. Yet, some still find they are not really happy most of the time. Some complain that even if they're not actively "fighting off" depression, still the major part of the day isn't spent in laid-back happiness either.

One man wrote me the following: "I was wondering whether you could tell me when depression has become a habitual state for a number of years how long it takes for Directed Thinking to become a habitual reaction? That is, how long does it take to lay down enough neural pathways so that switching the alarm system off is relatively easy to do, and being in a relative state of calm becomes more 'normal'."

I responded to him that the main neural pattern that you form is the *memory that reminds you that you can use mind tricks to get out of your depression.* This memory becomes linked to any depression that comes down on you. Now you never get depressed without the accompanying idea that you can now proceed to immediately get out of it. But the actual work of doing the mind tricks is still work, still an act of will every time, still a hard choice as opposed to the easy choice of succumbing to depression.

Directed Thinking never becomes passive thinking. What becomes automatic, through practice, is the ability to ignore depression once the edge is off. Remember, you must think depression for it to continue, and any thinking about depression is always passive. Any On-Purpose Thinking will immediately replace passive thinking. For myself, I always choose to do other things than think about my depression and after a while I just notice that it is completely gone.

Self focus is the culprit

The same man inquired: "Will depression stop being the dominant factor in my life? So that life is enjoyable and beautiful again? I guess it takes a little while until depression stops being there all, or most of the time. I find Directed Thinking a tough thing to do. But I'm doing it and I am functioning okay. But will it get easier?"

I responded to him that the big problem is self-focused thinking. Self-focus is the cause of all our anguish. People who have spent a long time depressed are just naturally prone to it. The answer to happiness is to get out of the habit of self-focused thinking. It must become your habit, instead, to continually turn your thinking away from what you are feeling to what you are doing; from disengagement to re-engagement; from an interest in your own happiness to being interested in other things and other people's happiness; from subjective thinking to objective; from "Oh, I'm not happy" to "isn't that an interesting pattern of light on the wall."

We think our feelings are our reality. But any thinking about how we feel is not present reality. To think about our feeling means we have to think about something already past which we must *replay as present*. Again, this is the reason depression is the opposite of living in the NOW. Self-focus is the opposite of living in the NOW. Life is always enjoyable in the NOW.

It takes a little while to get out of the self-focus habit. While you are doing this, *how you feel* must cease to be of such high importance. No matter how outer-directed your *action* may be, if you are always focused on what you are *feeling* instead of what you are *doing*, you will always end up feeling less than whole and happy.

Self-focusing constantly pokes holes in your okayness. It all ends up leaking away. You must learn to accept some amount of suffering as normal and move ahead with your day. When you live by feelings it is almost like you are trying to *make* reality instead of learning how to simply move forward in it. You must live the life you have, not the life you want. And the funny thing is, when you live the life you have, remain in present reality, you always end up wanting exactly what you've got.

When I get too self-focused on feelings it sometimes helps to look at the larger reality of my surroundings. For instance, I live on this planet spinning through space at somewhere around 1000 miles per hour. The resulting centrifugal force doesn't throw me and my car off the road because we're held down by gravity. My planet has a molten core and its surface, whereon sits my house, and all I love and hold dear, consists of tectonic plates that are in constant motion, causing earthquakes, volcanoes and pushing up mountains. We depend for our lives upon the sun which will some day swallow up the earth, or burn out; either way spelling the end of humanity as we know it. Now, what was the real problem I was worried about?

Don't lump your problems and your depression together

Most of our problems could be faced so much more easily if we didn't have to deal with our difficulties through the haze of debilitating anxiety and depression. Depression is different from a normal relationship with problems. When problems come we are *supposed* to suffer, just like when we cut our finger it is supposed to hurt. Think what kind of a human being you would be if you could not suffer?

But depression is different. It is different because of the stress chemicals involved. For millions of people depression *is* their problem. But for all of us, we may be surprised to hear that our perceived problem may not be *the real problem*.

The real problem may be that when difficulties arise, we allow them to become stuck to our depression like Siamese twins. Then, instead of working productively on our problems, we spend all our time worrying and stewing in our depression. I received a letter from a man who read my book *Depression is a Choice*. He wrote that although the book helped him tremendously in the past, he had a relapse of depression that was hard to manage because it was "this time around a more specific issue."

He had been diagnosed with a facial skin condition. "The condition is incurable and since I can't make it go away, it is very difficult to make the accompanying depression go away. I was able to manage my general depressive moods previously with some of the tips you offered in your book, but I am struggling immensely with this situation."

Here is another case of thinking you are suffering from your problems when, in reality, you are simply suffering from your depression. You can always stop depression with Brainswitching, and then you can bring more reason to bear on what problems you have.

Solving problems

Even if we are not able to solve a particular problem, by facing it honestly and rationally, we set ourselves on a path which leads us to the best part of ourselves. One of the most destructive things in our culture is an attitude that we are always supposed to be winners, that every problem can be fixed. This attitude is not only immature, it is pointless.

This side of enlightenment our very lives are coming at us in the form of problems to solve. Problems and Life are synonymous. Since the ultimate point cannot be to solve Life, the ultimate point cannot be to solve the problem either. So what is the ultimate point? Just as the point is not to solve Life, but to engage Life, and interact with Life, the ultimate point is to engage the problem, and bring our best to bear upon it, surrendering the final outcome to fate, instead of worrying that we won't be victorious. Then, win or lose, we win ourselves.

Ten

Depression and Emotional Dependence

The mind is not as smart as you think.

The mind is very powerful, but it is not as smart as we are because we have more options than our mind. How do we know this? No matter what thought happens to pop up in our mind/brain, if we want to, we can refuse to think it. We can decide to think another thought.

The mind does not have this option. Though our mind cannot force *us* to think its automatic thought, *we* can force the mind to think any thought we want! If the thought pops up, "I am sad today," we can refuse that thought. We can choose to think, instead, "I'm feeling just fine today, thank you very much! And in a few minutes, I'm going to feel even better." We can insist that our mind think this thought for as long as we want, choosing our on-purpose thought over and over. Sooner or later the mind will give up on its passive thought "I'm sad today."

When you realize that we don't have to think any passive thoughts that pop up in our heads, you can immediately see that we have the power to reject any of the mind's instinctive, automatic, emotional strategies. The mind's emotional strategies are thoughts, or feelings caused by thoughts. When we become aware of them we can refuse such strategies as anger, fear, paranoia, anxiety, confusion, and depression. The mind cannot force these strategies on us against our will.

Yet, there are those who maintain against all self-evident truth to the contrary, that we cannot get out of depression as an act of will. There is no proven scientific evidence that we cannot. It is simply a currently accepted medical theory that we cannot. The thousands of people now Brainswitching out of their depression are helping to change this attitude.

Let's not get all crazy with the theoretical orthodox

We get into trouble when we turn our eyes away from the practical, from the self-evident, from the proof of our own observation and experience. As a human being you have the capacity to recognize truth when it appears before you. You just have to be careful not to cover your eyes with fear, with borrowed wisdom, political correctness, or theory-based orthodoxy.

I would like to relate the following small incident in medical history. It's an illustration of how far wrong we can go relying solely upon "experts," and blinding our eyes to the practical and the obvious.

Conventional wisdom is not always wise

In the first half of the 19th Century there was no physical evidence of germs. We couldn't prove they existed, but of course they killed millions of us anyway. Puerperal fever (childbed fever) was as feared then as smallpox for it killed millions of young women.

In 1847, a young Viennese doctor named Ignaz Semmelweiss noticed that women in one section of his hospital had consistently less puerperal infection than women in the other section. The infection-free-section's babies were all delivered by nurses or midwives. The more-infected section's babies were all delivered by regular doctors or medical students. Semmelweiss observed two things: one, midwives were insistent upon absolute cleanliness; two, a hospital pathologist died (with the same symptoms as puerperal fever) after cutting his finger on a soiled autopsy instrument.

The right answer was so simple

Semmelweiss concluded that childbed fever was caused by "cadaverous particles," and decayed organic matter transmitted to patients by medical students who came to the maternity ward after doing autopsies on women who had died of childbed fever. He instituted the first hospital antiseptic procedures anywhere in the world. Medical students were told to wash their hands with a chlorine solution. The rate of puerperal fever seemed to decrease.

Of course to our 21st-century minds, sterile conditions in a hospital are elementary. In 1847, however, the established doctors flatly rejected the younger Semmelweiss's observations. He could not convince them to clean up. Instead, the physicians thought the increasingly frustrated Semmelweiss a certified lunatic, due to his yelling and screaming at them."For God's sake, wash your hands. You're killing them. You're killing them, you murderers!"

Semmelweiss became such a daily embarrassment to the medical staff that they convinced his family to involuntarily commit him to an insane asylum. He died there, just a few years before the work of Joseph Lister and Louis Pasteur established the germ theory of disease, which Semmelweiss had correctly intuited.

Isn't it frightening that doctors fought such an easy thing as washing their hands? But it seemed preposterous to them that such a simplistic solution as washing your hands could possibly be the answer to a disease that was killing millions of women. They saw no possible connection between the two things.

Even after Semmelweiss's raving exhortations to the contrary, doctors continued to deliver babies with hands still soiled from their autopsies on women who had died of disease. Because there was no "scientific proof" that it was in any way harmful, doctors were loathe to give up what were then considered badges of honor—-bloody hands and bloody aprons in which they paraded proudly from one patient to another.

Brainswitching to get out of depression is like washing your hands to prevent infection.

Brainswitching exercises are so simple that people tend to dismiss them out of hand. They couldn't possibly be the answer to such a serious disease as depression. But, although simple, Brainswitching is not so easy to do at first. To function from the neocortex, we must be proactive. Unlike the instinctive emotions of the subcortex, our full upper brain cognitive faculties do not just "happen" to us.

Full *emotional* thinking can erupt at any moment. Our tantrums can explode, anger flare up, depression or mania come upon us suddenly and full-blown. But if we want full-power *rational* thinking we have to "click it on," much like we click on the computer. We "click onto" our reason by deciding to use it. If we do not *decide* to use our thinking brain, then our emotional brain will continue to dominate and dictate our feelings and behavior, for good or for ill.

All children should be taught somewhere along the line, either directly or through role-modeling, how to choose reason over emotion. If they miss this important bit of psychological education, they never become emotionally independent. People who have no "hands on" practical experience in accessing their neocortex during emotional upsets may continue to throw two-year-old temper-tantrums right into senility.

Emotional dependence

Spousal abuse, for instance, is a case in point. The abusing person sees no other option but to "act out" fearful emotions and replay their emotional lives as if they were still a helpless, panicked child. These people inevitably blame the other person for "starting it" or "upsetting them." The truth is they have been upset all their lives because they don't know that their brain has two separate parts: a feeling part and a cognitive part, and that they can choose one over the other.

They have never properly learned to call on their reason during times of emotional turmoil, and consequently have never felt securely in control of their own lives. Since they are never in emotional control, it *seems* to them that whenever they get upset, it must *necessarily* be the other person's fault.

We say these people are emotionally dependent on their feelings because they cannot act independently of them. They cannot over-ride their anxiety, and rationally question their own thinking and actions during times of stress. This is a painful, fearful way to live, and emotionally dependent people often turn to alcohol or drugs to self-medicate, to "get a buzz-on" to cover the agonizing undercurrent of rage caused by their felt helplessness, the source of which they are totally unaware.

It is no surprise to a psychologist that spousal abuse happens in all socio-economic groups. A person may be financially independent, socially independent, even intellectually independent from "groupthink," and yet remain emotionally *dependent*. An emotionally dependent person cannot act independently of their own emotional turmoil.

Depression is an example of extreme emotional dependence

People who get stuck in depression have a dependent relationship to their thoughts in that they cannot think or behave independently of their depression. It *seems* to them, when they get depressed, that they have been attacked by a force over which they have no control.

Once a person understands how it is possible, by changing their thinking, to switch their neuronal activity from their emotional brain (subcortex) to their thinking brain (neocortex), their relationship to their depression changes.

When they realize their own thinking has caused their depression, they're no longer doomed to emotional dependence. They can think and behave independently of raging feelings. They can think and behave independently of both depression and anxiety. Anyone can achieve this.

Depression is different from spousal abuse, of course. But both are a case of emotional dependence that can be cured by a thorough understanding of how your mind works, plus some practice in accessing the neocortex when the subcortex has plunged you into emotional Hell.

Mania is also emotionally dependent

Mania is also emotionally-hooked behavior. The manic person does not recognize their thinking as separate from whatever emotion is raging. In general, a manic person does not have the perspective of knowing, even intellectually, that they have both an emotional and a rational brain. Therefore it is impossible for them to discern from which part of the brain they are functioning from moment to moment.

Take gambling as an example. A person who is not manic can gamble and, at a certain point of loss, make a rational proactive decision, independent of the urge to recoup, and walk away. A person in the grip of mania can lose their house in a game of blackjack.

A person who is not manic will choose to access the neocortex in times of stress, and make a decision at cross-purposes with their emotion at the time. For instance, they may be driving in a car and late to a meeting. The stressful thinking about being late may trigger the fight-or-flight response, causing stress chemicals to start pouring in. But instead of behaving their emotions—speeding, cutting off people on the road, etc. —they will start thinking more rational thoughts, "Okay, so I'm late. It's not the end of the world, etc., etc."

Mania gives a false feeling of power

A person in the grip of mania does not wish to access their neocortex in order to "go against" their subcortex. They like the subcortex being in charge. The subcortex, being our primal defensive instinct is linked to and rooted in our very survival. It's extremely powerful and when we identify with it, *we feel powerful*. So when we're late our mind is screaming that this is IMPORTANT. WE MUST GET THERE ON TIME. IT'S A MATTER OF LIFE AND DEATH. In going along with the subcortex, we feel important in what we are doing. It is a powerful feeling manics are loathe to give up.

Sometimes a manic idea happens, just by accident, to be a good one. But since the thinking and behavior is emotionally powered, and the emotion is dependent upon the stress chemicals which are very hard on the body, mania usually runs out of steam. At that point, the ball is dropped and there is no follow-through.

People wrongly think that it is wild emotion and rampant passion that create art, music, and literature. The subcortex does give *power* to us in the form of excited or fearful thoughts that produce the adrenalin to get us going. But to do anything worthwhile, we must direct our thinking away from our agitated subcortex by accessing the neocortex for the strategy and reason that allows us to persevere with our chosen goal *no matter how we feel.*

People will not be able to see their own mania until they have taken care of their depression. Once I had a good handle on depression, I no longer experienced mania as a powerful, beneficial high. I was able to see the fear and anxiety in it. It became almost as painful to me as depression.

Once you are educated to the workings of your brain, and psychological defense mechanisms, you can successfully manage your anxiety, depression, panic and mania instead of being terrorized and made ill by them.

Eleven

Depression: You Think It, You Feel It, You Behave It

Your thinking, feeling and behavior are not something you are, they are something you do.

It is helpful to compare depression and rational thinking. Rational thinking involves real proactive decisions. If you look very closely you can see that all the action you take concerning chronic depression is *reactive*, out of fear. If you make a long-term habit of reacting and responding, after a while it no longer feels like "your life."

The action taken in rational thinking, being proactive, can be based upon some chosen goal, some deeply-held principle or some guiding precept. In other words, rational thinking can be for love of something. But "love of something" should not be confused here with feelings.

A person who lives by feelings can drive themselves crazy trying to choose between two things; not knowing which one will pan out in the long run, to "make them happy." This is because emotions are fear-based. Another problem is that emotions tend to push us towards the specious and quick, rather than the measured and profound. In decision-making you shouldn't be looking for immediate results, you should be looking to be *appropriate* at each instant. Appropriate is not a feeling.

If I have learned anything in my life, I have observed that nothing good comes ultimately from anything I've done out of fear. If there is one standard I would use to base any decision on it is this: whatever you do, make sure you are doing it for love of something rather than fear of something.

Nothing you do out of fear will be appropriate to your life, because it will not be a real proactive decision but a reaction to fear. Depression is always a reaction, it is never proactive. At no time can something prevent you from being proactive in your thinking. Not even a depressive episode!

Real decisions are not out of fear

To make a decision with courage, for the love of something, is always a real decision. Most people fear a real decision because it always involves risk. *A real decision is the opposite of a guarantee.* You may lose something. But generally the loss will be appropriate in some way to your life. Conversely, you may make a decision out of fear and "win," but what you win will almost always be *inappropriate* to your life in some way. The highest reward for good decisions is not what you get by making them, but *what you become* by making them.

Suppose you have just started dating a man who wants a sexual relationship right away, and you are not ready for that kind of commitment. You have to make a decision. If you engage in sex out of fear to lose the relationship, you might keep your boyfriend. If you opt out of sex, to be true to your own standards, you may lose him.

It's not always easy to figure out if you are doing something out of love or fear. In the above case, for instance, it will be tricky to figure out if your decision to have sex would be based on love of your boyfriend or fear of him leaving you. Which of the two is the salient reason?

To make a proper determination, it will help if you acknowledge any fear as it comes up, experiencing and using up the fear "in the raw," so that it doesn't become a hidden impetus. In the above situation, one could feel how scary it would be to lose your boyfriend and be all alone, and maybe never find someone else. One should attempt to feel this fear physically, in their body. The other tricky thing is to accept the fear, rather than just feel it.

Feeling your feelings and accepting your feelings

There is a big difference in *feeling* your feeling and *accepting* your feeling. Acceptance usually comes with a relaxing of the body. It may be that relaxing the body on purpose might even assist you with the acceptance. If there is such a thing as a "core, or real self" that people are always talking about, it is probably the self that has been hemmed in by unacknowledged fear, unable to come fully forward. It is very exciting to discover, within yourself, the self that has always been there beneath the fear. For myself, I liken it to the words of an old spiritual—"peace like a river in my soul."

It will also help to make a right decision if you can separate the decision from some kind of ultimate win or loss that might depend upon the decision. For instance, in the above situation, you need to separate out the necessity for keeping your boyfriend (winning) from influencing the correct choice of whether or not you are going to have sex.

All real decisions involve risk and therefore courage. This is the true definition of courage, isn't it? Sticking to your chosen principles in the face of your fear. Difficult decisions can show you the difference between courage as a real goal, and courage as an idea—a figure of speech that lacks substantive relevance to your life.

Whatever time you have to ponder a decision, it should all be spent figuring out if you are deciding something out of courage, out of love of something; or fear of something. This discussion about courage may seem like a digression from depression. But it is important to illustrate how much you can learn about yourself by being aware of what kind of thinking you are doing.

As you observe your thinking, you are able to see your thinking more as a tool for your use, rather than confuse your thinking with you, yourself. Your thinking is not something you *are*, it is something you *do*. Understanding this, you can learn to disengage from the kind of thinking that leads to depression, and initiate the kind of thinking that can get you out of it.

You know those little downward thrusts of feeling that indicate depression is imminent? If we're not careful how we treat these incipient feelings, our *thinking predictions* of coming agony can insure their accomplishment.

Once deep into depression, it seems a difficult journey from the feeling that "nothing is possible" to "everything is possible" again. Yet it is not a great journey for it can happen within the confines of your own mind. It is the journey from the small isolated subjectivity of the subcortex to the larger common ground of present-reality possiblity in the neocortex. Remember, if you are emotionally hurting, you are not in present reality. You are in your subcortex. You have to get out of the subcortex and into the neocortex so you can re-engage with life.

Disengagement is both the problem and the solution

Some people mistakenly believe they are forced by depression to disengage *from their regular lives and normal activities.* They don't see how they are *choosing* to withdraw, and that they could make another choice. At first they might not "feel like" doing something. But this feeling can be overcome and in doing some small thing, depression will already start to weaken. Very often, insight in some small thing can shed light on our larger reality.

We might notice, for instance, that in the completion of some small task we have not thought about our depression for 2 or 3 minutes. Unless you simply give yourself up to depression immediately and never consider making any choices, you might begin to notice that the path out of depression always involves some kind of either/or choice.

For instance, you don't need hope if you refuse to think about your despair. You might see that you cannot appreciate something and be in pain at the same time. These insights, unfortunately, are not the easy intellectual type. They are experiential. In order to be experiential you have to start paying more attention to the thinking you are doing at the moment. Become a participating observer. Soon you will be able to see the choice-forks in the road instead of running, willy-nilly any-which-way, as your pain impels you.

You will start to realize that in withdrawal from activity, you unwittingly welcome and set the scene for depression to move in and settle down. You will begin to understand that we withdraw and disengage because we *feel* like doing it, not because there is any true *biological* imperative. Without due diligence, however, you won't get this. You won't "get" that depression is not so much a state of mind as it is a choice of behavior, instant by instant.

It helps to keep remembering that depressive behavior is something we do. Therefore it is something we can *stop* doing. Depression is not a physical symptom of a serious illness, like a fever or a rash. It is more a self-vicious form of learned helplessness. Depressive behavior is a habitual routine of disengagement from regular life. It is a routine of subjective, self-focused, passive thinking which leads to the triggering of the fight-or-flight response, and the production of stress chemicals which effects appetite, sleep, etc., leading to extreme physical agony.

The power of a daily routine

It is very interesting how some pharmaceutical companies have cleverly co-opted these habitual depressive routines and natural body reactions to stress chemicals into the *diagnostic symptoms* of depression that it purports to cure by drugs.

Unfortunately, pills may give you some relief, but they don't give you any skills. With Brainswitching exercises you begin to form strong coping mechanisms that can get you out of depression quicker and quicker as you practice them. Depression as a major focus of your life will start to retreat out of the foreground. It will be easier and easier to focus your attention away from incipient worry.

You'll start being able to stick to small alternate routines, even boring morning rituals, instead of thinking about your depression. You will find that, little by little, these routines will replace the depression, and then you will start to *enjoy* the routines. You will have come back to life. Life was always there, but you couldn't connect to it while you were depressed because life is always in present reality and depression is always in the past.

Finally you will find it is a wonderful thing to get up in the morning and be able to live in the world as you find it, and as you find yourself. You are the "you" you have always been. But you will feel like a different person because you have made the leap from the past to the present, from chaos to order, from potential to actual. Even the trees and the sky will seem more colorful.

Even if you wake up depressed you will be able to get going on your day *anyway*.

Anyway

It seemed like a miracle the first time I realized that no matter how depressed I was that I could get on with my life, *anyway*. Then I started thinking about the word itself. Anyway. And I realized how powerful and prophetic that word is. *Anyway. Any way.*

The secret to handling depression lies hidden away and shining like a lost gold nugget in that one word, anyway. Any way. Any single, small thing we do when we are depressed immediately serves to weaken our depression because depression is the idea that we can't do anything. But we can. No matter how depressed we are, we can do something else other than our depression, anyway, any way. Like all roads lead to Rome, any way leads us out of depression.

Of course it also helps to stop beating yourself up!

We all have sore spots in our minds, just like we have sore spots on our bodies if we have fallen, or been cut or bruised in some way. We have learned to avoid the sore spots on our bodies. We can see it is simply not rational to purposely push against some cut or scrape and make it hurt. But some of us haven't learned to avoid the passive thinking that pushes against and agitates the sore spots in our minds that can pitch us into depression.

When we learn to recognize our sore spots we can choose not to think them. We choose not to think them by thinking something else instead of them, so they can't get a place on our attention span. These negative, self-abusing thoughts never disappear. They are always latent in the memory system of our minds. But latent thoughts can't hurt us. Dormant thoughts can't hurt us. We don't have to kill them or drown them with drugs. Only thoughts that we actively think can hurt us. The bad news is that we activate those thoughts ourselves through passive thinking. The good news is that we can immobilize them ourselves by Directed Thinking and Brainswitching.

We are not a victim of circumstances

It is *our* anxiety, *our* tension. After our fight-or-flight response has been triggered, and the stress chemicals start up, and we disengage, and become non-responsive, then it becomes *our* depression. We are the maker of it. No one else made it but us. This is good news really. What we have built in our ignorance, we can now proceed to tear down with our new knowledge and understanding. Remember, ignorance just means "to ignore."

In depressive self-focus we have allowed old disturbing thoughts from our memory banks to continually replay themselves to our rapt attention. We have been seduced and hypnotized by them. We have let our mind be carried along by whatever repetitive idea or feeling randomly showed up. Then, through learned association, more and more disturbing thoughts have compounded themselves until we have found ourselves deep within our own painful, passive thinking. Our fight-or-flight response spews out the stress chemicals. We're trapped.

But there is a way out. *An on-purpose thought can get us out.* This is the whole idea of Brainswitching and Directed Thinking. Once you have chosen a non-stressful thought, and think it repetitively, the mind will stop passively hooking up with the stressful thoughts through learned association. The mind will change its direction and, through learned association, start hooking up with *non-stressful* thoughts. An on-purpose thought always trumps a passive one. The door to truth will start to open.

Remember, the mind moves in the direction of *our* most current **dominant thought**

When you're depressed, your dominant thought is a passive one. You need to change that, and make your *dominant* thought an on-purpose one. You make a thought dominant by choosing it over and over, repetitively. Depression is caused by self-focused thinking that is automatic and mechanical. Like any instinct or impulse, we do not have to call upon self-focused thinking for it to appear. Any negative, stressful thought can think itself, repetitively, if we do not choose to interrupt the repetition.

But we *can* interrupt the stressful repetition anytime we choose, by thinking some non-stressful thought. Remember, since the brain is a thought-thinking machine that's almost always turned on, it is almost never *not* thinking, even when we're asleep. And because the brain (and its product the mind) is instinctively a *defense mechanism*, the mind's default position is always negative. We get the mind out of automatic passive-default thinking by choosing, repetitively, a neutral on-purpose thought.

The power of a thought

Brainswitching is the most efficient antidote to depression because nothing works faster than a thought to power your brain. It is a neutral thought that can bring immediate neuronal activity to the neocortex. Drugs take weeks, or months. Talk therapy takes weeks, or months. A thought takes an instant.

You just need to remember that you are the one that determines what your dominant thought will be: passive, or on-purpose; positive or negative; subjective or objective; neocortical or subcortical. You can always over-ride your mind's random and instinctive thought choice. Again, you have free will. You are not forced to function from instinct (the subcortex), you may choose to function from reason (the neocortex). You can decide if you want your current dominant neuronal activity to be mainly in the subcortex or mainly in the neocortex by the current thoughts you choose to think. This gives you the capacity to reject any impulse, no matter how strong.

Our thought is our choice

Long-term depression is caused more by faulty thinking than faulty chemistry. We are a biochemical entity. We can choose our thoughts, and there is a chemical consequence in the brain for every single thought we think. It is one thing to think a thought. It is a far different thing to choose to think a particular thought.

People with depression and anxiety are usually so self-identified with their thinking that they don't see themselves as separate from it. Therefore they don't see themselves as being able to direct their thinking. They don't break the thinking process down to see that their thinking is made up of thousands of disparate, if similar, thoughts every minute.

The thinking process is made up of a succession of thoughts. It is easy to see that you are not simply a thought. It is an easy step from here to see that if you are not a thought, and thinking is a bunch of interconnected thoughts, then you are not your thinking, either. If you, as a human being, cannot be limited to one thought, you cannot be limited to any combination of them either.

Now you might counter by saying that our body is made up of atoms and we can't separate ourselves out from our atoms. But we can't change the order of our atoms around as an act of will the way we can change the order of our thoughts as an act of will. In this way our thinking is similar to any part of our body that we can activate as an act of will, like moving an arm or a leg. We identify with our emotions more than we do with our arms and legs. We know our arms and legs aren't "us." And with some effort we can begin to see that our thinking and emotions aren't "us," either. Exercises #1, #5, and #9 in Chapter 19 are helpful here.

The very fact that you can change it any time you want, should be the absolute proof to you that you are not your own thinking. When you see you are not your thinking, you can see that you, and you alone, have control over your thinking. We are *not* our own thinking because we can *choose* our own thinking. Whatever it is about us that chooses our thinking, is much more powerful than just the thinking itself. Therefore we do not have to be a victim of our thinking. Since our thoughts determine our feelings we do not have to be a victim of our feelings either, up to and including depression.

Twelve

Dangerous Thinking

Only someone who is in charge of their thinking is in charge of their life.

When I say "we should be in charge of our thinking and our thinking should not be in charge of us," everybody nods their heads in agreement. People think that, of course, they are certainly in charge of their own thinking. But wait! If we spend a long time anxious, worried and depressed, that means our thinking is in charge of us!

There still doesn't have to be a problem even if this is true. Brainswitching can maneuver our minds out of anxiety and depression. But once the edge is off our depression, there is a whole life to lead. If we want to live it less frantic and more laid-back, happy, we need to become more aware of the kind of thinking we do that leads to anxiety and depression. Then we can turn back from it early on, and move our thinking in another direction—toward calm. It has been said that depression means there's no light at the end of the tunnel. We can't see the light because we're looking in the wrong direction. We need to turn around.

The reason we don't realize we can turn around is that, unfortunately, most of us don't inquire much into our thinking. It's as if our thinking is something automatic that can very well go on without us. We pay such scant attention to the process and content of our thinking, it's almost as if *what* we think is none of our business, and we shouldn't meddle with it. But there is a kind of thinking that's extremely dangerous, and we *should* meddle with that.

Beware of passive thinking

Repetitive, passive thinking can magnify distortions we might be making. We've all heard the truism about "say something often enough and people will believe it to be true." We are all susceptible to this kind of deception. It's human nature. Advertisers have exploited this for years.

There's even more danger in *self-deception*. If we *think* something often enough we can come to believe it is true. Since others are not privy to our thoughts we are less likely to get a clue from others as in the case of some wrong notion on television. Our neighbor might voice some credulity about something on television we believe to be true and then we might question it as well.

It's harder to question our own ideas. We can become so totally cemented to our exaggerated notions that we lose the ability to think and behave independently of them—which means we also become defensive about them. Which means we become stubborn, conceited. Conceit is just another word for defensive. Humility is the opposite of defensive.

Some thinking may be out of touch with reality

There is no one more imperious and unaware than a chronic victim of exaggerated thinking. Without some mind management on our part, any one of us can become a "Chicken Little," convinced that our own sky is falling.

We can become so dependent on our wrong-headed ideas that if someone questions *them*, or our depression, we mistakenly believe they are questioning the worth of our being. Trapped in a delusion of our own making, we lose the power of acceptance, of humility, of self-questioning. We are stuck in the grip of anxious worry. But we don't see it as anxious worry that *we are doing*. We see it as anxious worry that is somehow *doing us*.

Passive repetition of the thought "I am depressed" can imprison us in such a way that our painful thinking becomes our only reality. The door to truth is always there, but our own self-focus slams it shut in our face. When this happens we are just as isolated as if we were on a desert island. We have little emotional connection to the regular events of our lives, nor to the people around us. We just drift around in the grey fog of our own self-fusion. We feel victimized by something over which we have no control. In truth, as a result of the kind of thinking we allow, we are the author of all that we are feeling.

We should avoid some kinds of thinking

Some kinds of thinking cause us to disengage from our regular life and live temporarily in a private world we don't share with others. In our shadowy world of depression, for instance, nothing's worth anything, and we feel empty and hopeless. We think this is reality. We think this is necessary. We certainly don't see this as some kind of a thinking option.

This is the biggest problem with not questioning our own thinking. *What* we think begins to have *credibility* with us simply *because* we're thinking it; that it *must* be a true thing. But as the 16th-century philosopher Michel de Montaigne warns us, "Men are apt to believe what they least understand." This is especially true about depression. People believe in it fervently. Not as a thinking *option,* but as their absolute reality.

If we understood more how our mind operated, we would not be so overly impressed, and so easily overwhelmed by the painful, fearful, or bizarre thinking that suddenly engulfed us. We wouldn't jump right up and salute it, as some kind of inexorable reality, as some "necessary" beingness into which we must now collapse, body and soul. This is particularly true of depression.

Just because depression erupts doesn't mean we have pay it any attention. Except to note that we don't want to go there, we want to turn around RIGHT NOW and go somewhere else in our mind. When depression happens, it doesn't mean that we have to *think* it at all. Depression is the most misunderstood event in the whole psychological industry.

Depression is unnecessary thinking

Depression is unnecessary, subjective, self-focused, passive thinking. The thing that most people don't realize about depression is that depression cannot think itself. *We* have to think it in order for it to continue. If we choose to think something else *instead* of it, depression will immediately lose its power. Its pain will start to fade as the stress chemicals cease, because we are no longer thinking the stressful thoughts that trigger them.

When we understand *how* we think, and become more wary of *what* we think, we are able to see things as they *really are*, rather than how we *feel* them to be. At this point we will no longer see depression as a solid reality, but as temporary, optional thinking.

We don't have to think our depression

Free will, remember? We can always think something else instead of depression. We can always escape to the neocortex. This is why it is so important to know the difference between thinking and feeling so that you don't mistake what you are feeling with what is objectively the case.

Deciding what is feeling and what is thinking is not always easy at first. We need to observe our feelings and thoughts as they occur so we can be more aware of which is which.

When we're depressed we *feel* our life is hopeless. *In reality* our life is not hopeless. Other people around us can see that, but we are separated from that present reality because of how we are using our brain, or maybe I should say how we are *not* using our brain.

It's not that I want to "blame the victim" here. What I want to do is assure you that although you can't help getting that initial hit of depression, you don't have to stay long in it. It is not what it seems. There is a part of you, the neocortex, that will not feel all is hopeless. You need to get to your neocortex to see that you have options; to reconnect yourself to present reality.

How do we judge reality?

This is a very important point. If we think of depression as an option, we can make a choice to get out of it. If we think of depression as an incurable disease, we won't make a choice to get out of it. Things are often not what they seem because our mind is not necessarily a clear window to reality.

We do not see present reality *through* our minds but *with* our minds. Our minds constantly restructure reality for us according to what we already know. We judge every *present* situation according to the *previous* experiences we have already imprinted in our neurons. Or as the famous saying goes: We don't see things as *they* are we see them as *we* are. This is why a toddler doesn't see any danger in a busy street and we do.

We also see things according to borrowed knowledge. We assume a thing is true if we trust the person who tells us it is true. If our chemistry teacher tells us a certain compound will kill us if we were to put a bit on our tongue, we would just plug that knowledge into our brain without testing it out for ourselves. A teacher or a doctor, for instance, can tell us things that we simply accept as fact, and live our lives accordingly from then on. If a doctor tells us that our depression is an incurable disease that will come and go for the rest of our lives, we tend to believe it unless we have other information to the contrary

Sometimes when a doctor gives you such a diagnosis, he doesn't give you any other information to the contrary even though it might exist. Sometimes a doctor does not explain depression in terms of how the brain works. I picked up a brochure on depression from my local hospital. It says: "no one really knows what causes depression except that it is associated with low serotonin." Believing that depression is caused by lack of serotonin is like believing the rain is caused by the lack of sun just because whenever it rains, the sun is less visible. Not all borrowed knowledge is true but people can live their whole lives *as if* it were true.

The way we see depression and anxiety depends upon what we have already programmed into our mind by way of our own learning experience and education, and what knowledge we have borrowed from others. This is how some people can get out of depression quickly. They see it differently. They see it as passive thinking they are not compelled to do because they can immediately choose to do Directed Thinking. When depression punches, they counter-punch with Brainswitching. Take that! And that!

Mind exercises "at the ready"

I have 4 or 5 mind exercises that I always have "at the ready" in case depression suddenly hits. Sometimes I use "row, row, row your boat, etc." Sometimes I use "yes, yes, yes, yes." If one exercise doesn't seem to suit me at that moment, I quickly choose another, and I keep up a steady pace of repetitive thoughts until I notice that the edge is off the pain. Even with the edge off, I'm still not feeling all that great. But the extreme death-like agony no longer paralyzes me.

That endemic gloom that no light can dispel is loosening its grip. I continue with Directed Thinking, getting into morning exercises or chores, then quickly taking up the day's work, concentrating on what I am doing and avoiding thinking about what I am feeling. I think objectively. I notice little things in my environment on purpose: the way the light shines in a window, the way books are piled on a table. I avoid subjective, self-focused thinking about myself.

For example, if I am suddenly engulfed in the subjective thought that I feel terrible, I grab for an objective thought. Even if it's as simple as concentrating on the weave of a sofa pattern. Objective thinking, apprehending some physical reality, like the sofa, with one of my senses, sight, takes me out of self-focus and puts me in present reality.

I remember, deep into the worst depression, that passive behavior and disengagement may *immediately* be changed, *as an act of free will*, for on-purpose, productive behavior. So I immediately do it. You can immediately refuse depression, not the feeling, but the behavior. With different behavior, the feelings subsequently change as well.

Specifically, if they pop up, I ignore my mental sore spots. Oh, I know them so well. They want me to think them so-o-o bad! But I turn away. Sometimes I even say to myself, "Oh no, I'm not going there!" And I mentally turn my back and choose some other path of thinking that is more objective, productive and rational. In this manner I take on the day, and generally notice somewhere into my mid-morning activities that the depression has totally gone.

Since rational behavior of any kind has a calming effect on emotions, the latest medical research now concludes that prescribing physical exercise is as effective for depressive episodes as medication. For the same reason, physicians in Great Britain routinely prescribe self-help books for mild to moderate episodes, instead of medication.

Social anxiety is also a product of passive thinking

When I am at a party I sometimes start to feel alienated and unappreciated. People begin to seem cold rather than loving and accepting. When I catch myself feeling this way there's a little trigger thought that says, "Uh-oh, I must be self-focusing." I immediately start paying attention to someone else and turn my focus 180 degrees about. If I bomb out with the first couple of conversations, I persevere. I don't care if I end up talking to the waiter! I keep on until I get a good conversation going where I am interested in the other person instead of myself. You get better and better with Directed Thinking and Brainswitching the more you practice it. You become more and more in charge of your life.

It is good to be clear about what, exactly, you are thinking

If you practice sorting out your thinking and earnestly want to know what you are up to, thinking-wise, you will find out. When you are aware what kind of thinking you are doing, process-wise (whether it's passive or on-purpose, subjective or objective, etc.), then you'll be able to check out your thinking content-wise as well (what exactly am I confused about?). There's another factor in being able to see reality, to see things as they really are. If we are frightened in some way, we might devise a way of looking at some things that shields us from seeing the truth. I watched my eight-year-old granddaughter do this very matter-of-factly. There was a scary scene in the Wizard of Oz movie that we were watching. All of a sudden she twisted her self around on the sofa and told me, "I'm looking at it upside down so I don't really know what's going on."

The very language we use can subtly distort reality. If we would be more accurate in describing things, we would be able to make better decisions about them. If we called it sugar water with poison gas in it instead of a soft drink, maybe we wouldn't drink so much of it. If we called it gambling, instead of gaming, maybe we'd think less of it.

The 19th-century English jurist Sir James Fitzjames Stephen said, "Men have an all but incurable propensity to prejudge all the great questions which interest them by stamping their prejudices upon their language." Psychiatrist Thomas Szasz put it this way, "We use words to label and help us comprehend the world around us. At the same time, many of the words we use are like distorting lenses: they make us misperceive and hence misjudge the object we look at."

Advertising agencies use language to con us into doing what they want, whether it is in our best interests or not. Used cars are called previously-owned cars. The emotional feelings engendered by certain words can subvert our rational processes. Nobody wants a USED CAR while everybody wants to OWN A CAR. You can see the different feelings inspired by the two different phrases.

You see ads for a WHOLE half of a chicken. You get the emotional high from the word WHOLE so you kind of ignore the fact that you're only getting a half. A sales manager once told me he never asks a customer to "sign something" because, "Everybody's mother has warned them never to sign anything, and they will immediately get skittish and resistant." Instead, he presents a contract and asks the prospective buyer to "please authorize this." Everybody wants to have authority. Authority is a *good* thing.

In the same vein, if we call depression a disease, we can be convinced that all we need to do is to take medicine for it. We will feel no need take any other personal action on our own behalf. We will not grow and mature emotionally as human beings as long as we allow ourselves to speak this language of convenience. I say language of convenience, because truth can be extremely inconvenient. Truth generally requires that we ourselves have to get busy and do something difficult.

Thirteen

Where There's a Will There's a Way

The elect are those who will, and the non-elect those who won't.
— Henry Ward Beecher

Many psychiatrists have been telling us that we can't help ourselves because depression deprives us of our will. This is not true. Depression does not deprive us of *will or option*. It merely deprives us of *motivation* due to the heavy toll the stress chemicals wreak upon our metabolic system. If depression deprived us of will, we would not be able to do so much as to lift up our own arm. Will is not quantitative. It is qualitative. *Motivation is quantitative.* It is the feeling of *wanting* to do something, in degrees of more or less.

Depression per se does not really limit our behavior. There's nothing you can't do while being depressed. You still have the *will* to do whatever you want, even if you don't *feel* like it. You do other things as a matter of will that you don't *feel* like—writing a report, getting dinner, doing the laundry. *You just haven't applied this same principle to depression.* Mainly because some people in the psychological community have you convinced that you can't.

You can opt out of depression

Once we believe something, it is human nature to discount contradictory information as incorrect or irrelevant. Therefore it's hard to get out of depression, as an act of will, when people we respect tell us that we can't.

Getting out of depression is harder than getting dinner or doing laundry, admittedly, but the fact remains that it is *just as doable.* Especially if you are alerted to the difference between will and motivation. Even in the depths of depression, a person still has the capability to change their behavior at any moment. It is a *simple* enough thing to stop crying and do some little exercise or mind trick. It is a simple thing to take your attention off bad feelings and concentrate your attention, instead, on the weave of the material on your sofa. It isn't *easy,* because you lack motivation. But you *can* do it when you remember that you still have will, *free will.*

It's tough to take action when depression first hits because you have almost zero motivation. But if you remember you still have *will,* still have capability, you will not be fooled by the strategy of your depression to render you helpless by depriving you of motivation.

Remind yourself that you have *will* often enough when you aren't depressed and can concentrate on it fully. Then you can start to build a neuronal thought pattern that will show up on its own, triggered by learned association, because you have linked it with your depression. When depression hits you will feel the same pain but a new thought will occur to you, "I still have will, and I can do an exercise and get out of this." This is just one example of how you can physically change your brain by changing your thinking and behavior.

Anticipate the tricks of depression

We need to *anticipate* our belief that nothing can be done when depression hits. Then we won't be so easily seduced by it. Deep into depression it is impossible to believe that you can do anything to fix it. That is the very core strategy of depression, *complete belief in your own infinite helplessness.* It's hard to tell whether helplessness causes the low motivation or vice versa. Nature's way of protecting our earlier forms has backfired on modern Homo sapiens.

We have this brain with its elaborate human psychological defense mechanism, and all its biochemical bells and whistles. But it has evolved from that ancient stop-do-not-go-forward-danger-ahead program and the *stop* is still there, preserved in depression. We immediately withdraw and surrender. *Knowing* our first instinct is to stop, to quit and go belly up, can help us override the primal directive.

The trick is to decide, *in advance,* that you will automatically *substitute your new exercise for the missing motivation* whether you *feel* like doing it or not. We should not live our lives by *feelings* anymore than we should drive a car without a steering wheel. Feelings power us but they have no sense of direction.

Doing trumps believing

Depression is the belief that nothing will work so why do anything. Therefore, just 60 seconds of thought-jamming it with "green frog" will start to lessen its strength. When we decide to slip another routine in on our regular depressive routine, it begins to lose its power. Depression is a mindset, a mind channel. You don't need to cure your mind; you need to change the channel.

The only thing you need to cure is your habitual reaction to depression. There is no reason to cure depression at all because you can simply walk away from it, via Brainswitching mind tricks, to a different place in your brain. Lacking the proper thinking fuel for its survival, depression will then subside into its cyclical downtime.

Doing the exercises will physically change your brain, neuron by neuron. There in your brain, right next to your path *into* depression, will be your path *out*! This is why depression no longer frightens me. I'm very aware of my well-built path out of depression.

Visualize it: two neuronal thought patterns in your brain. One is your regular routine of depression and one is some routine of mind exercises to get out of depression. Both patterns will always be there. Once you form a neuronal thought pattern it never goes away. That is a problem with depression but it's a good thing for your exercise program. Ease up on your depression routine and begin to use the exercise routine instead. Then the depressive routine will not be forming as many *current* learned associations as the exercise routine will.

Living in the NOW

We might not see it ourselves (although our friends and loved ones can certainly see it), but too many of us unwittingly *choose* our pain over our life. We do this when we choose the past over the present. This creates the illusion that causes us to believe the symptoms of *not* handling our depression are, instead, *caused* by our depression

Depression is the opposite of living in the NOW. You could almost say it is our *punishment* for not living in the NOW. Living in the old neuronal patterns of our depression is not necessary, and it doesn't help fix our problems either. And then we think our problems are causing our depression. To be accurate, we are never depressed because of our problems. We are always depressed because of our depression. Problems can only be fixed in the NOW, in present reality. Depression and anxiety are not present reality. Whenever we are depressed we are no longer in present reality.

How do we get from depression to NOW?

NOW is neither a time nor a place, it is a way. Any decision you make, no matter how small, puts you immediately in the NOW. Life is always a task, done or not done. Life is always a risk, taken or not taken. We are always, upon every moment a "yes" or a "no"; an "is" or an "is not"; a "now" or a "later." The difference is decision.

How about negative decisions?

There is no such thing as a negative decision per se. There are poor and wrong decisions as events later prove them because we don't always know all the facts. And besides, no one is immune to stupidity. So decisions may be negative as to outcome and content. But decisions are always positive as to process. Here's another way to say this.

The act of making a decision is always positive even though the decision itself might have negative consequences. This is the problem with alcoholism. The initial decision to take a drink is positive as to process, and makes us feel in charge, even though it is negative as to consequences as we become drunk and out of control. Once we understand the importance of decision as regards to process then we make better and better decisions as regards to content. According to research, proper-content decisions are a problem for people who are depressed.

Depressed people seek the negative

Depressed people avoid favorable feedback and positive situations and actively seek negative feedback and negative situations. People who are depressed tend to engage in behaviors best described as learned helplessness. They habitually employ weak, monotone speech, unresponsive body language, and flat facial displays just so they will get negative feedback from others to reinforce their negative self-view. (*Journal of Abnormal Psychology*, Vol. 105, No. 3, pp 358-368.) Why would anyone do this?

It makes perfect sense when you think about it. Being a herd animal, we all need to feel connected to others at a core level. We get this sense of belonging by a self-validation process which has us searching our immediate environment for that which mirrors our self-concept, our sense of self, our truth.

It is basic human nature to seek confirmation of one's own self-views. When we are depressed, what is our self-view? Nothing we do makes any difference because life is hopeless and it's always going to be that way. This idea is simply incorrect, but we don't realize that it's an idea because we have confused our feeling and our thinking. Unless our consciousness is raised to a higher awareness of the difference between thinking and feeling, we always believe our feeling as reality.

So what can we do when we're depressed to avoid seeking the negative? The answer is that we can opt for the power of positive behavior. We have to recognize the real reason we don't want to do anything, so that we can move beyond it. We have to go against our first instincts to seek the negative in order to self-validate. We have to move against our comfort zone when we're depressed and engage in productive and positive thinking and behavior which is not necessarily self-validating during a depressive episode.

Feelings are often wrong

Have you ever considered that there is sometimes no reason to pay attention to, much less believe what your brain is telling you when you are depressed? There is a lot of nonsense and old story-telling going on in there: life is terrible, nothing is worth anything, why bother, I'm depressed, I can't get going.

You've heard these old thought patterns for years, that's why they seem so "you." But they are not you. Your brain is your brain and you are you. You can think any thought you want. Your brain can only think what is already in its memory banks—what pops up via learned association. And it can't even do that if you insist on thinking something else instead.

Unlike the automatic workings of the brain, *your thinking choice can come outside of instinct and learned association.* Your thinking choice can come from a book, or from a wise person. Your mind cannot refuse to think any thought if you decide you want to think it. But you can refuse to think any thought you want. You can render any thought powerless by your refusal to think it. You always have two options, think or feel what the brain pops up, or think whatever thought you want, in order to indirectly get yourself to *feel* however you *want* to feel.

As you exercise the thinking behavior you want, it will become stronger because it will be engendering more current learned associations. You will become stronger, more solid in your thinking, less able to be sidelined by depressive and anxious thoughts that pop up. As physicist Stephen Hawking said, "The degree to which a particle is likely to wander in an indeterminate way from the straight and narrow is determined by its lack of mass."

Fourteen

Can We Really *Think* Our Way out of Depression?

Life is the story you tell yourself. Make it a good one!

The antidote to the risk of taking responsibility and facing our own fear has always been to find safety in an excuse. *People behave differently when they are responsible.* If they feel "insured" by excuses for risky behavior, their behavior tends to *be* risky. This has two outcomes. First, one makes no essential progress in building coping mechanisms because one does not make the best use of one's resources. Second, as our belief in personal responsibility goes down, our belief in freedom goes down and we start to feel boxed in and paranoid. If all environmental issues are property rights issues then all mental illness issues are *freedom issues.*

Unfortunately there's a huge excuse out there, for the taking, which is boxing in millions of people. A current generally-accepted medical theory about depression is that we are helpless to do anything about it as an act of will. *This provides a big excuse in the sky for everybody.* We do not have to take responsibility for our own depression. We can blame our chemical imbalance, our neurotransmitters, our problems, our excess of epinephrine.

We get no *good* out of these excuses. Well, ask yourself how it *profits* you that you are not responsible? A wise person does not pursue a road that offers no profit at the end of the journey. Excuses do not offer psychological salvation. When you know how your brain works, you can start to see that we are wholly responsible for what we think or feel.

Since this is the case, it means that you are a free person to the exact extent that you take full responsibility for your thoughts and emotions. The reality is that whether you take responsibility or not, you have always *been* responsible. *The human spirit cannot be excused from evolving.*

We think, at first, that an excuse frees us from something. It doesn't. It ties us up. Keeps us from becoming our best selves. Weakens us. *An excuse is not a ticket to anything.* It is a kind of prison of the soul.

Where did this depression excuse come from?

When people are depressed, doctors can point to their brain scans and see that all the neuronal activity is in the subcortex, the *emotional* part of the brain. Very little neuronal activity is in the neocortex, the *cognitive* portion of the brain. This is wrongly interpreted to mean that depression must be a brain disease. What they are ascribing to pathological neural brain activity might better be attributed to one's thought *choice*. Let's use some common sense and logic here. What does neuroscience really tell us?

- Certain thoughts cause neural activity to spark up in the subcortex; other kinds of thoughts cause neural activity in the neocortex.
- If you think emotional thoughts, the subcortex is going to light up in the brain scan as neurons get busy passing around information.
- If you think neutral or nonsense thoughts, the neocortex is going to light up for the same reason, increased neural activity.
- A human being can think any kind of thought they want at any time.

We can see, neuroscientifically, how we think our way into depression. How is it so difficult to imagine how we can think ourselves *out of it*? It absolutely can be done. We just have to remember that Directed Thinking doesn't appear on its own. We have to initiate it as an act of will.

We do this by giving the mind a task. Any kind of a task, simple or complex. Accessing the neocortex is a qualitative not a quantitative process. The reality is that either you do it, or you don't. When you understand that depression is just your psychological defense system gone off by accident, you'll be surprised how proactive you can become.

Brainswitching gets us to experience, maybe for the very first time, that we can have an *immediate* effect on our moods by manipulating our thinking. In persevering we become sturdy, confident, grounded. We can see how it is possible to get our brain to do what *we* want, not what *it* wants (based upon old habit patterns).

Our brain is a de facto defense mechanism. It is our brain that "wants" depression and anxiety because they are a byproduct of the fight-or-flight response. We cannot do without a strong, well-functioning defense system. But we *can* do without depression and anxiety. *We* do not want them and *we* do not have to put up with them. We must go on the offensive with Brainswitching when our brain goes defensive on us.

Feelings are not rational

In order to be successful with Brainswitching, we must get some practice in distinguishing between feeling and thinking. Subcortical feelings are defense mechanisms; they should not be mistaken for neocortical rational thinking. Feelings warn us of danger but *they can be wrong*.

Essentially, depression is wrong. You feel that your life isn't working. However, as soon as you change your depressive *feeling*, even though nothing else about your life will have changed, indeed you will see that your life does work.

When we are depressed, we have only a one-way communication with our mind. Our mind is telling *us* what to feel and think and do. We need a two-way communication system. We need to think the thoughts that engender better feelings. As far as the brain is concerned, we can insist on a baseline competence, feeling-wise. Depression can be vanquished.

We give depression all its power; *we* maintain the length of our depression by thinking about it. Yes, depression can trigger off automatically by learned association beneath our level of awareness. But spending hours, days, or weeks in depression is not something that happens to us, *that* is something we *do*. We can learn to *not* do it.

Interstitial choice

Even though Brainswitching absolutely works, neither thought choice nor "Freedom of the Will" is *easy* when you're depressed. If you substitute any neutral phrase for the thought "I am depressed," the pain will lessen. You can certainly choose a nursery rhyme, or grab for some repetitive phrase when depression hits you, anytime you want, without further instructions.

But, for those of you who require a more intellectual explanation before you are willing to try any exercise, I include the following breakdown of choice as it concerns choosing a thought to get out of depression. Remember, this information *is not* necessary for you to do Brainswitching. It merely breaks down choice so you can study its parts. But it is also complicated and rather boring to explain so feel free to skip it if you want to.

The anatomy of choice

Brainswitching is a very quick, small and invasive choice. Although the choice, per se, is simple, it's hard to do because it first involves the awareness that there is a difference between you and your mind. I call it *interstitial choice* because it depends upon this difference, this small psychic space between you and your mind.

Choice, as it concerns choosing a red car over a blue car is easy to see because a car is only one thing; we are not fooled. Choice, as it concerns feelings, is different. Feeling is like a mental optical illusion wherein two things appear to be one; we can be fooled easily.

We cannot see through this illusion *intellectually,* but we have to consider *the concept intellectually.* Then if we "hang out" with the concept, and practice the mind exercises, we will start to get little hints for ourselves until a new fork in our regular thinking path appears suddenly before us, and we can take a quick sidestep that will make us suddenly discontinuous with our depression.

The optical illusion of feelings

Here's how to get past the optical illusion of feeling. First, we have to realize that feeling consists of *two* parts. There is the biochemically-based feeling itself, *then* there is the bioelectrically-based *thought* that we-know-we-are-feeling-it.

The only possible way to employ judgment in the neocortex is if we know, first, that we are feeling something. Before we *become* happy, we must first know we're *feeling* happy. Before we *become* depressed, we first have to know we're *feeling* depressed. There is the further elaboration of *we know* that we know.

Ancient wisdom says that human beings are sentient because, not only can we know something, we also *know* that we know. An important point is that *what* we know changes, and *that we know we know* never changes.

We know when we suffer depression because we are suddenly in pain. That's a change from *not* being in pain. We notice things when they change. *That we know we know* we are in pain is not painful, and our attention is never drawn to it because it never stands out. It never stands out because it *never changes. Feeling* is one thing. *Knowing* that we are feeling is another thing. *Knowing that we know* is different still again.

Knowing that we know

There are many kinds of knowledge, like knowing feelings, or knowing mathematics; but there is only one kind of *knowing that we know.* As concerns depression, there is a tiny window of opportunity between the *knowing that we feel,* and the *knowing that we know.* It is rather like splitting the atom to see that space between knowing something, and knowing that we know. But a most powerful opportunity exists within that split. That is where you find *choice.*

We don't have trouble choosing between a red and a blue car. How do we, exactly, choose between depression, and not having depression? Here is the answer. The instant we know we are *feeling* depressed we must remember there is another kind of knowing, where we *know* that we know. It is this place which gives us the opportunity of choice. We can choose a neutral or nonsense thought that will *replace* the neocortical thought "*I know that I am feeling depressed*." Now we can know a different thought instead of knowing we are feeling depressed.

Interrupting the progress of depressive thought

If we keep ourselves from knowing we are *feeling* depressed, we can keep ourselves from *becoming depressed*. When we realize we can always interrupt the progression from *knowing* that we are feeling depressed to *becoming* depressed, we will no longer see depression as choice-less. We just need to *know* some other thought, like the words of a nursery rhyme, instead of *knowing* that we are feeling depressed. When we choose *not to know* we're *feeling* depressed, we therefore won't "*get depressed.*" It is a mind trick.

We never know something without *knowing that we know it*, but we usually focus on the *knowing something* part instead of the *knowing that we know* part. We don't need to know *that we know* in order to feel our feelings or carry on the intellectual work of our lives. But, in order to transcend and direct our feelings, which we want to do when depression hits, we need to focus on *knowing that we know*, because that, precisely, is where choice lies.

We can kind of "hang out" with this idea that there is a place where *we know that we know* until it "falls" into our awareness. This place of being is always the same, no matter what we are *feeling*. However, it is all-enveloping, so obvious, and so never-changing, like silence, that someone first has to alert us to look for it. The old philosophers used to clue us in on this kind of thing. No one knows they are missing awareness, until someone points them to it.

A more cosmic awareness of choice

We do not need to suffer long if we change our focus from knowing *what* we feel or know, to knowing *that* we feel or know it. The mystic George Gurdjieff called this "self-remembering." Nisargaddata Maharaj called it "the witness consciousness." It is not the kind of awareness we can do "on the fly" with our daily busyness, trying to multi-task half a dozen things. We must come to a complete STOP. Becoming an aware person is probably one of the non-busiest things to do; because it's not a matter of effort. It's a matter of being awake, silent, and leaning on "a way" until we "fall into it."

The practical experience of choice

Practically speaking, for depression, here is the self-talk we can do. "Uh oh, I know I am feeling depressed, and I would rather know *something else* instead of this feeling, so I'm choosing to know something else, like "row, row, row your boat." Choice will not only shift the increased activity of our neurons from the subcortex to the neocortex, but it will thought-jam the awareness of the depressive thought in the neocortex. This is the simple mind trick that takes care of depression. It is simple, but very hard to do at first. However, anyone *can* learn to do it.

Fifteen

The Exercises

Our mind already knows how to direct us. We have to learn how to direct our mind. Our mind already knows how to trick us into believing that moods are reality. These tricks are the natural consequence of evolutionary eons of our psychological defense system—the fight-or-flight response. We have to learn how to proactively trick the mind out of its primal, instinctive, reactive moods so we can disconnect from depression and reconnect with present reality.

Depression is an automatic biochemical strategy of the brain. The brain can't help doing it. But *you* can help it. You can move away from habitual, meandering mindsets. You can let that kind of defense-mode, anxious, fearful and guilty thinking go right on by you like a parade, without getting emotionally hooked into it. We needn't be gobbled up by our own negative thinking.

The exercises here will help accomplish this. There is no reason that we should let depression turn our own mind into our worst enemy. Mind exercises teach us some psychological space between us and our emotions.

Emotions are not present reality

A friend once said to me, "It is hard to reach people where they hurt because we are more attached to our suffering than almost anything else we know." The psychological term for this conundrum is "enmeshment." It is human nature for us to self-identify with our emotions as if they were our objective reality.

We don't see how we actually withdraw from objective reality, fleeing into the arms of our very seductive and often painful emotions as if they were the real world, our motherland. Then suddenly we feel trapped and isolated in the fog of our feelings and, for all intents and purposes, we have withdrawn from the real world.

Emotions are strange for the very fact that they are not necessarily connected to any "real world." If you think about it you will realize that chosen principles are always connected in some way to the real world. Principles allow you to function rationally, and, generally speaking, more productively.

Emotions are just the opposite. They hinder you from productive functioning. True, in the form of stress chemicals produced they provide power to initiate action. But the sooner you stop focusing on your emotions, and focus on your chosen goal, the better off you will be. All great athletes understand this. They are reasoning how, specifically, they are going to make the next play. They are not worrying about winning or losing the next point.

The more emotional and subjective we become, the less real and objective seems the outside world. This is how we can believe our lives are terrible and hopeless when, in fact, it is only our *feelings* that are terrible and hopeless. We don't see we are clinging to our feelings, instead of pursuing other present possibilities that are much more real and solid than our feelings.

Objectivity helps

Psychological exercises and mind tricks can give us a break from our feelings. They can let us rest for a moment in a kind of *benign objectivity*. They help us set our problems down every once in a while, so the heavy thinking about them will not further trigger the production of fight-or-flight stress chemicals.

Mind exercises can give us some space between us and our habitual negative mindsets. Often something magical can happen in that space. Either a new idea or a new acceptance emerges. Exercises establish new neuronal connections in the brain that we can later grab onto for emotional balance in times of stress and panic. These exercises help us make concrete physical changes in our brain patterns that indirectly bring about changes in our brain chemistry and our moods.

No matter how deeply into our moods and mindsets we have allowed ourselves to sink, these exercises can help us climb out. The mind can give a depression or a panic, and we do not have to go. We can do exercises instead, until the panic and depression fade of their own accord.

Well, they don't really fade of their own accord. They fade as a direct result of our learning *how not to aid and abet them.* Exercises train the brain to develop bypass strategies we can take, just like an elevator, out of the insistent downward pull of painful emotions. We're not repressing feelings, you understand. We don't want to do that. We are changing thinking so that different feelings will emerge.

The mind is supposed to be a tool, not a trap

We can begin to see the mind as a mechanism, rather than mistake the habitual workings of particular mindsets for the totality of who we are. Exercises break the habit of getting sucked into our feelings, and give us a wider and more efficient natural perspective from which to see the world and function in it.

The mind should be a tool for our use. We should not be a tool of the mind. Our lower brain may "feel depressed," or "anxious," or "panicky." But we don't have to feel that way. Our brain should be the continually changing and improving result of Directed Thinking and doing. We should not be the result of our mind's passive thinking and doing.

Fear that has been triggered, either by real or paper tigers, needs to be used up. Irrational, non-specific, or imaginary fear has the same chemical effect on the body as real fear. We must channel unused fear, the fear that has not led naturally to some action, into some kind of physical or mental exercise that can complete the fight-or-flight syndrome. Then the body can return to its more normal non-stress mode. Mind tigers cause real stress. Mind exercises *cure* real stress.

Stress relief and more

Exercises can benefit us in ways that we might not be able to imagine beforehand. They can help relieve stress, depression and negative thinking. They can give us enthusiasm and renewed hope in the face of our difficulties. They can provide self-understanding during times of confusion. Some of the mind tricks are like magic time capsules that get our brain to consistently build up small neuronal links of positivity that can be accessed during times of stress and anxiety

Each of us is a unique person, and at any moment our stand in life is not, and cannot be, duplicated by any other human being. So we are the best judge of which exercise might work for us at any particular moment, simply because we are inexplicably drawn to it at that time.

Mental gymnastics are not so different from physical ones. When we flex our arm muscles, or our calf muscles, we can see, physically, wherein lies our power to move around and do things. Although most people never think about the possibility of doing so, we can also flex our mind "muscles," and see wherein lies our power to think, feel and do what we want. Our mind is the same as our arm and leg muscles in that we strengthen the parts we use most often, and the parts that we don't use become weaker and weaker.

Sixteen

Brainswitching Exercises

Brainswitching exercises are the best first aid for depression. They are the first thing you should reach for when depression hits. The important thing is to prepare them ahead of time so you can use them immediately. The quicker the better.

EXERCISE #1: GREEN FROG

Choose a word or phrase, such as "green frog," a nonsense nursery rhyme, or song to have "at the ready" the next time depression hits. Simply concentrate on that single thought, the poem, the nonsense rhyme. Anything will do. "Row, row, row your boat." "One two, buckle my shoe." Insist. Insist! Insist!

This is such a simple, dumb little exercise that, at the outset, it seems too trivial in the face of the horrors of depression. But it works miracles, as many simple things do. When we exercise our imagination, we start the neurons arcing in the neocortex, the seat of all our creativity. A human being can only think one thought at a time. When we concentrate on any neutral thought, the anxious thought "I am depressed" is temporarily blocked from our attention. When we cease to pay attention to our depression, it cannot think itself.

Even done out of spite it works

Even when people do this exercise out of spite just to prove that "such a stupid thing couldn't possibly work," it still works. Just the cognitive thinking that "the dumb exercise won't work" is enough to distract our attention, even for a few seconds, from our concentration on the thought "I am depressed."

As you practice this exercise, your powers of concentration on your chosen thought will improve over time so that your depression will have less and less power to suck you in, and dismantle your equilibrium.

Bad feelings should alert us to use first-aid Brainswitching such as "green frog." Then with "green frog" thinking in place, thus blocking thoughts about feeling bad, slowly get busy with chores or regular duties, followed by more ambitious work. The new activity will spark up neurons in the neocortex, and cause the slowdown of neuronal activity in the subcortex lessening the stress chemicals being poured into the brain.

When one is well into productive behavior and thinking, then the chemicals dissipate, and the edge of the emotional trauma will be taken off. We will start to notice some rise of our essential okayness. There is always some productive work that can be done, even cognitive thinking about what small tasks one might look around for if none come readily to mind.

There is no reason to endure agonizing feelings more than a few minutes. But no time should be spent on wondering why the bad feelings occurred. They are always the result of some pattern of thinking, some learned associations that have connected in your brain. Any maverick thought could be the trigger: cloudy day, the color purple, some sad song. It doesn't matter. The obvious task is simply to change our thinking, and then the feelings will change to reflect the new thinking.

We usually don't give importance to the fact that what gets us down, and let's face it our moods change though our situations remain the same, is the fact that our brain is essentially a defense mechanism. It allows us to survive a basically hostile cosmos. Humans are fragile. A rock doesn't have much need for a self-activating defense system.

EXERCISE #2: JUST SAY YES EXERCISE

Say "yes, yes, yes, yes, yes,yes, yes, yes, yes, yes, yes, yes, yes, yes, yes, yes, yes, yes," over and over to yourself. You can do this for 2 or 3 minutes straight, or longer. If you use this in the morning before rising, then immediately after the exercise get busy on some small chore that will set you going about your day.

Once we learn language, we *self-talk* in our minds all the time just beneath our level of awareness. When thoughts are not naturally directed to some ongoing, productive activity, our defense-mechanism mind starts looking for no-no's in our path. When we get depressed for "no reason," it may be that we have unknowingly been saying "no" in our minds for hours. Each separate "no" is a little neuronal link to trains of thought that are negative, or fearful, in our minds. Our brain can become a stress chemical factory due to the alarm that "no" sets off.

Probably the first terror we felt as a small child was somebody suddenly yelling at us "NO. NO. NO. Don't touch that." The thought "no" is probably all we need to start the old fight-or-flight chemical alarm going.

Imposing the positive

This exercise doesn't solve anything "out there." We are not saying "yes, yes" because we like anything that is happening at this moment. It is just a mind trick. The "yes" which we are imposing on our mind has an inherent effect on the brain neurons which is just the opposite of the "no" which our defense mechanisms may have imposed. An on-purpose "yes" is a natural antidote to an autonomic "no." As the "yes, yes, yes," thought replaces the "no, no, no," the chemical factory starts to shut down.

One of the things that I rather expected "yes" thoughts to do would be to activate, by learned association, other positive thoughts; thoughts associated with "yes" kinds of things as opposed to "no" kinds of things. This would start more neuronal activity lighting up in the neocortex. I was sure I was right after the following experience occurred to me.

I often wake up with last phrase of a dream in my mind that doesn't make good sense. Sometimes it is a sentence I am saying to someone in my dream. I get weird snatches of conversation all the time. Things like: "It's a cipher with a physical residue." Or, "So that is how you keep it from becoming an entrophe?"

What happened this particular morning was that I didn't feel very well when I first woke up so I grabbed for the "yes, yes, yes" to distract my mind from thinking I was feeling bad, so I could construct a better mood for myself.

Then I fell asleep again for just a few minutes. I wouldn't have been surprised, having gone to sleep thinking "yes, yes, yes" to have awakened thinking "yes." But, instead, I woke up thinking "on, on, on." Which certainly can be associated with the word yes, as in onward and upward, keep on, etc. And also, "on" is the opposite, mirror image of the word "no." Very interesting.

A positive could trigger its opposite

Except for this "yes, yes, yes" exercise, I don't usually suggest positive thoughts or personal affirmations for Brainswitching and thought-jamming since, through learned association, a positive thought, *could* trigger its opposite negative one. Positive thoughts and affirmations are very valuable as a quick follow-up to Brainswitching.

I really like this "yes" exercise and use it all the time. When really anxious, I use "yes, yes, yes," followed by some variation of the Emile Coue affirmation depending upon what immediate problem I'm struggling with: "Every day in every way I am eating healthier and healthier food," or "Every day in every way I'm feeling better and better."

I also find this exercise helpful when I wake up at night agitated by some problem, or just before I go to sleep. It is a great device for thought-jamming painful thinking, to keep it from being the focus of my attention.

EXERCISE #3: PRAY FOR SOMEBODY

You may be very good at this already. I was not. I had to figure out how to do it. I visualized the person troubled over their situation, then I imagined myself taking their hand, or whispering in their ear, "I am with you, you are not alone," or "Please let me help you bear this terrible pain." If they were struggling with something, I imagined that I was telling them to "go for it" or whispering "You can do it." If sick, I sent angels to minister to them, carrying the proper medicine. I don't know why, but my angels were always small and white. This exercise helps to get our mind's focus off our painful feelings by focusing our attention on someone else. And in the great scheme of things, who knows. Perhaps our prayers will do someone some good.

EXERCISE #4: PILOT OF THE MIND

When you find yourself sucked into the deep nose-dive of depression, visualize yourself sitting in the pilot's seat of a plane. See your hands grabbing the controls. See the black plastic wheel in front of you. Now pull forward and go up, pull forward and go up, pull forward and go up, up, up. See the nose cone of the plane pulling up out of the steep dive down and begin to climb up, climb up, climb up. Out of the dark into the blue sky and sun.

EXERCISE #5: PUT OFF UNTIL TOMORROW

We needn't buckle under to depression. Depression is the *idea* we're helpless, not the *objective reality* that we're helpless. When depression is just starting to come down on us, if we are quick and proactive, we could decide to just "put it off." We could tell ourselves, "Oh yes, it's coming, but I can do my exercises first before it gets all the way here." Or, "I'll just check my email first before it gets too bad" or "vacuum the rug." If we put off that ultimate surrender to depression with small activities that we do "first," our direct neuronal path to depression gets interrupted. We get better with practice. Forcing simple activity, *whether we feel like doing it or not,* often deters depression entirely. When we get busy with something *else* our brain "forgets" about depression. When other neuronal pathways are activated, depression is deprived of necessary "juice."

Seventeen

Directed Thinking Exercises

Directed Thinking exercises can build a calm, confident center in your brain by building nourishing neuronal thought patterns which you can then use instead of the painful, destructive patterns that lead to anxiety and depression. These exercises will provide a new fork in the road that you can take instead of the path that leads to depression.

These exercises do not need to be done in any order. Try one. If you make a commitment to one exercise and fail, just reaffirm the commitment and start again. If one works for a while, and you want to drop it for another, nothing will be lost.

EXERCISE #1: A BIT OF LIGHT IN THE DARK

Here is one of the mind tricks I created to help me see my moods more objectively. When I was depressed and feeling low, I would visualize "saving some of it in my hand" to take into the next high, to "remember" how I was when I was down. This was not terribly difficult. And when I was feeling good I would "save some of it in my hand" to take into my depression to "remember" how it was when I was joyful. This was much harder.

Since depression by its very nature is "hopeless," it necessarily seems "endless." Thus, it is hard to remember "being up" in the midst of a down, with the implication that another up period will also come. But I insisted on doing the exercise and slowly, little by little, I got to the point where I could hold onto the *idea of both extremes* as being *temporary moods*. Switching from the *idea* of one mood to the *reality* of the other, back and forth, back and forth, regardless of which mood I was in, I learned to feel my strongest feelings without losing my sense of objective reality that *I was not my feelings*, I was simply having them. I learned to raise my awareness and observe myself carefully when I was deep in depression, being careful not to get to the point of *experiencing myself* as depressed. One day my depression was separated out, and I was outside of it, looking at it.

EXERCISE #2: THE NEXT TASK

When we are in despair we feel helpless and there is nothing to hang on to. There is no feeling of security. We feel so lost, as if the ground has just opened up, and some great chasm is about to engulf us. This is very fearful. It is paralyzing. We don't know what to do. We don't *feel* like doing anything.

We *should* do something because doing something is the very way out of our despair. But what? The answer is that we can always do the *next thing*. There is always some small next task that we could do: pick up a book, water the plants, pay a bill, put our shoes away. Anything, just to get us started again. Once we have moved into the first task, the second task will become even more obvious. We won't *want* to do this. But we *can* do it.

If you really think about it, the fact that there is always a next task is comforting. It is comforting to be able to count on something that will never disappear. It is security for our sanity. We can always do the next thing. And it will always be there waiting for us. Like a trusted friend. Forever.

EXERCISE #3: THE OBJECTIVE PYRAMIND EXERCISE

On
This day
I will get up.
I will choose a task
I will begin right now.
I will gather my strength.
I will do the best that I can.
I will think only about what I am doing.
I will refuse to think about how I am feeling.

EXERCISE #4: THE TALISMAN

There is something very solid and believable about the material world, about something wood, or glass or metal that you can hold in your hand. A material object is, well, very objective. It is something we can use to counter-balance our subjective feelings when they are highly agitated.

We might forget that we can use Brainswitching when we panic, or are dumped suddenly into depression. We might forget that we won't *want* to do Brainswitching to get out of depression, but we should do it *anyway and any way*.

Some kind of talisman might trigger us to remember the objective reality that we always have a choice to get out of depression. It might help us to recall that we are not *really trapped and helpless* at the moment, that it's our *subjective* reality.

Buy a necklace, a bracelet or pin that you always carry with you to remind yourself that you are not ever helpless, that you always have choice. I bought a small sterling eagle on a chain, once, to remind myself. I used it for a year or two until I had built up sufficient neural patterns in my brain which would trigger off at the same time my depression hit and remind me. Since I had no further need of it I gave the necklace to a friend. A few years later, when she had no further use for it, she offered it back but I told her to pass it on to the next fellow traveler on the path.

EXERCISE #5: IT'S NOT AN OPTION

What is the world's most pointless activity? Thinking a negative or painful thought. As soon as we realize we are thinking some discouraging or stressful thought, we can say to ourselves, "There is absolutely no good thing that can come from thinking this thought. There is absolutely no good reason to think these terrible things. Even if these things *are all true,* it does me no good, and it does nobody else any good, for to me to think them. Thinking these things means I am doing self-focused thinking. Self-focused thinking is the road to Hell.

Why should I keep thinking that I feel bad? There is no earthly reason to think such a thought. Therefore I will not think such a thought. Instead of thinking 'I feel terrible', I will think 'I am feeling better and better, better and better.' Instead of thinking 'my child is hurting' I will think 'my child is getting better and better.' Instead of thinking 'I am going bankrupt,' I will think, 'the money is coming. The money is coming.' Instead of thinking 'The house is a mess' I will think, 'The house is getting cleaner and cleaner.'"

This is not a housekeeping exercise. This is a mindkeeping exercise. This exercise is to sweep away the pain that is caused by stressful thoughts. The mind can only think one thought at a time. It can't think its anxious thought if we insist on some other thought. We just need to get going and think it.

We can outsmart the mind and easily get it to think our thought. The only hard thing about it is to *actually do it.* Anybody is smarter than their own bad thoughts. Oh, sure, if we are going to cower in fright, and be a helpless victim, depression will gun us down without mercy. Why show ourselves to depression at all? Why not keep out of its way by escaping to the neocortex, where depression can't go. All we have to do is Brainswitch for a few minutes, and we'll be up in the neocortex while depression, stress and anxious worry will be down there in the subcortex all by themselves, without us.

EXERCISE #6: FOUR FRIENDS

When you're depressed and unable to get out of bed, imagine that there are four other people somewhere in the world, right at this very minute, who are suffering just as much as you are. Visualize these people straightening their shoulders, taking a deep breath and getting up and going about their day. One may be a teacher, a soldier, a mother, a newspaper boy. See them, one by one, starting to get busy, even though they are hurting just like you are hurting. Imagine one of them turning to you, smiling, and putting out a hand to help you up. Maybe they need your energy too. Maybe the entire world will be just a smidgeon better because you get up today.

EXERCISE #7: THE WITNESS TO DEPRESSION

Visualize the scene of a woman seeing her psychiatrist. She is sitting in a comfortable chair, in front of his dark wooden desk. The woman looks familiar, like someone you know. She is wearing a gray dress. The psychiatrist has white hair and a long white beard. He is looking at her very kindly, with great interest. She is looking terribly sad and depressed, even though there is nothing in her life to account for this overwhelming feeling of despair.

Imagine the psychiatrist turning to you and asking you, "What does she think?"

Imagine your answer is, "She thinks she feels bad."

Imagine the psychiatrist asking you, "Could she think something else?"

Visualize this woman deciding to think something else instead of thinking she feels bad. You, as the witness to this woman's depression, can see how she could make a decision to think something else.

EXERCISE #8: GO TO THE FIRST THING YOU CAN SAY YES TO

To stay in a negative "no-no-no" mind means that we will be stuck for a long time in depression. We are paralyzed because the mind is a "yes" system. It is a simplistic thing to say, but, to stay in a "no" mode is simply the lack of our decision to go to a "yes" mode. Once you know how your mind works, depression is simply the lack of a decision to be cheerful.

"I want to feel good," we wail. Then we must first *think* good. The first time I did this exercise I was so distressed. I racked my brain for someone or something I could feel positive about. My children, yuk. My husband, ugh. I was desperate. If you're shocked by my attitude, remember that when we're filled with fear and terror, and looking for help, we want a no-questions-asking, purely nourishing, not-wanting-anything-for-itself "sure thing."

Probably why we prefer the company of trees when we feel all is lost. A tree doesn't want anything from you. We're so low in energy we don't have anything to give. Which is why coming up with a positive thought seems impossible, even if we have the intellectual understanding we need one in order to get out of our dire straits. If we don't have the idea already programmed in our heads that we must bestir ourselves in this direction we generally just give up when depression hits, do nothing, and stay stuck down in the black hole.

This particular day I was going through my mind for possibilities to which I might give a positive thought. At last I lighted upon my dog. I thought maybe I could manage a positive thought about my dog, could give a "yes" to my dog. A small start but it worked. It's possible to switch our mind from "no" to "yes" this way and start the neurons sparking toward a more productive mindset through the process of learned association.

This is not a new idea. Salesmen know if they get a customer to say "yes," the law of inertia will work in the favor of the sale. There will be a small resistance in the mind of the customer, due to inertia, to change the "yes" to a "no." So the first question of all those telephone solicitors is "How are you today?" They expect you to respond with a positive answer, "Fine, thank you." "Is this Mrs. Jones?" "Yes." Thus the salesman sets the neural connections going which will lead to the "yes" of a sale. When we're in a down mood, we can "sell ourselves" on creating a better mood for ourselves.

Here's the exercise: Think of anything or anybody that you can say yes to, give a positive thought to. The first step out of our "no-mind" is to find something, anything, we can say "yes" to.

EXERCISE #9: REALITY CHECK

When you are in depression you are never in present reality. Test this out by engaging yourself in a conversation reality check. Ask yourself questions about exactly what is wrong "right now, this very second." You will find that your fears are always either anguish or regret about something in the past, about what you have lost; or fear about the future, and what you are not going to have. Any time you start to question yourself seriously about your exact concrete situation, you can always see that *in this exact instant* you are really "not so bad."

EXERCISE #10: LET'S PRETEND

If you can't relax, *pretend* to relax. If you can't laugh, *pretend* to laugh. If you can't be happy, *pretend* to be happy. Why? Usually you can't do these things because they are in opposition to your feelings at the time. But if you pretend, your brain will not know the difference, and your feelings will begin to mirror the pretending. All of a sudden you won't have to pretend anymore. You will be relaxed.

EXERCISE #11: PRACTICE THE POSITIVE ANYWAY YOU CAN

When you are deep in depression, it is practicing the positive to simply take a walk, make your bed, brush your teeth, take a shower, straighten up your room, or your desk. Being depressed means that you are already deep into practicing the negative. When you do the *smallest* positive thing, you have turned yourself completely around, 180 degrees, in the opposite direction. This is overcoming a lot of inertia, so your *second* positive act will already have been made easier. Even if you can't get out of your bed, and therefore don't have the help of physical exercise to focus on, you could still make a mental yoga room in your mind and do mental exercises. It changes the backward momentum. It starts to move you forward. Any forward movement is away from depression.

EXERCISE #12: PRACTICING SCALES

I am indebted to my friend Sofia Shafquat for this exercise which I have permission to repeat in her own words:

"Yesterday the pool-cleaning man told me he did not think life was worth living. He said he hated himself, and he was getting more tired of it all each year. I gave him my "scale" from 0-10. 0 being suicidal and 10 being joyful/ecstatic, 5 being 'no feelings at all.' I told him I had learned to gauge throughout the day where I was on the scale, and once I knew whether it was 3, or 4, or whatever, I could find a way to bump myself up ONE POINT.

This could be done instantly by appreciating something— the comfort of one's shoes, for instance, or the color of a plastic paper clip. And then you could bump yourself up another point by finding something else to appreciate even more. And before you knew it, you could find yourself in the positive range of the scale, above 5, and this was how your life would begin to transform. Garbage in, garbage out. Appreciation in, appreciation out. It has worked for me. The pool-man was astounded. He told me he could see the scale right there in his mind, and he knew he could use it all the time. He told me it made complete sense, and that he had always known how depressed he was, but he had never been able to come up with the 'initiative' to change. Now he saw how he could make a difference in his own life.

The funny thing is that I almost went to my usual pool yesterday, but at the last minute decided to drive to my 'old' pool, which I almost never go to anymore. Why?? I think I was meant to cross this pool-man's path and offer him this small thing." A small scale, literally, but with big implications.

EXERCISE #13: REMEMBER THAT YOUR BRAIN IS LISTENING

Your brain believes every word you tell yourself. Be careful what you say. You may need to stop using some of your favorite phrases like: "It's a pain in the neck," "I can't stand it," or "I don't want to hear it." Through learned association your brain will put in motion what it can to make what you say a reality. I warned my husband that he was going to go deaf because he kept saying "I don't want to hear it." A hypnosis professor of mine said he was sure that his wife's cancer of the foot was because she was always saying, "I can't stand it."

EXERCISE #14: BE GENTLE WITH YOURSELF

Say this over and over to yourself, *"Be gentle with yourself. Be gentle with yourself. Be gentle with yourself."* At the same time do the "Shoulder Drop And Back Release" (Chapter 20, Exercise. #1)," and "Crack the Great Stone Face" (Chapter 20, Exercise #2).

Clay E, a retired hospital administrator, told me that after his 23-year-old son committed suicide he would sometimes experience overwhelming feelings of grief and despair that would hit him suddenly "like a kick in the stomach." He would leave important meetings, not able to continue. He couldn't sleep, couldn't get up and go to work, couldn't take pleasure in his normal activities. One day the phrase "just be gentle with yourself" occurred to him. He felt calmer, more accepting. He got into the habit of saying it over and over to himself whenever his grief and depression overtook him. Such a simple device but a most powerful and spiritual one.

My friend has shared this phrase with many others who have used it to escape from their own anguish and despair. It is not simply the *idea* of the phrase that works, however. It is the *use* of the phrase; the thinking of the phrase instead of the thinking of the despair. The mind is very much like a frightened child at a time like this. We need to tell the mind that it is not necessary to beat itself up. The mind doesn't know this unless we tell it.

EXERCISE #15: THE MORNING MEDITATION OF MARCUS AURELIUS

This is the inspired mind trick of Marcus Aurelius, "In the morning, when thou art sluggish at rousing thee, let this thought be present. I am rising to a man's work."

EXERCISE #16: THE EXERCISE OF PRINCIPLES

Principles can save us from falling into stress, anxiety and depression. Not by believing in them, but by *using* them. As 18th-century English poet Edward Young counsels, "Let us cling to our principles as a mariner clings to his last plank, when night and tempest close around him."

The difference between emotions and principles is this: Emotions are autonomic defense reflexes. They have no inherent good or bad to them. We can't choose them directly. But principles are either inherently bad or good. We can't choose what emotions and feelings impel us. We *can* choose which principles we grab for when we're impelled.

Feelings can happen to us without any decision on our part. But principles are inert without our decision to use them. Feelings and emotions, even depression, are not problems in themselves. It is when we become helplessly subservient to them that they are a problem. Principles can keep us from becoming subservient.

Principles can be simple things. A small principle of "doing something" when we are depressed is more powerful than the overwhelming choicelessness of depression. If we're depressed and make ourselves do an exercise, this is principles-based action. We should not forget that choice is the most valuable thing we own. And yet how many people who are depressed simply don't see any choices in their lives?

Depression is fearful, yes. But human beings can deal with fearful things. We can decide to make the fear of not exercising our principles so paramount in our lives that it can guard us against any fear or depression that would *keep* us from exercising our principles. This is the training every soldier receives. The fear of *not doing his duty* becomes more important to him than the fear of battle. We should consider ourselves soldiers; we battle for our very lives when depression rises up to conquer us.

EXERCISE #17: SORTING THE MAIL

I received a letter recently from someone who offered me another great exercise. So here it is, in his own words. John Winston Bush, Thank you.

"I have a metaphor akin to your garbage truck exercise which I call SORTING THE MAIL. Most mail these days is junk mail, just as most of our thoughts are junk thoughts. Imagining going through the pile of one's junk thoughts helps de-literalize and dis-identify with the worst of it."

EXERCISE #18: SHREDDING THOUHTS

I find this exercise especially helpful when I'm trying to get to sleep and it's hard to get my mind free from its restless thoughts. I imagine my thoughts coming up out of my head and taking the shape of big paragraphs written on large pieces of paper. Then I let the paper paragraphs rise up slowly into a giant shredder which turns them into white confetti that whirls all around and falls softly like snow. Thus the thoughts are destroyed before I can think them.

EXERCISE #19: REFRAMING TO SEE THE TRUTH

Think and then reframe. What is going on in our psychological lives or in our relationships that we are not calling by the right word? We might call ourselves shy instead of scared. If we admit to being scared, we can call upon our courage. We might say we don't like conflict when it might be more accurate to say that we are *wimping out*. If we see we are wimping out, we would have the opportunity to decide to be more honest and forthcoming. Being right might be our justification for being just plain mean. If we catch ourselves being mean, we can decide to be more loving.

A little more about wimping out and being shy. You can get into trouble if you don't show yourself, if you don't' speak your own truth. People will not like you very much if you never speak up and say what you want to do, or what you think about some subject. In the first place they can't trust you because they don't really know you. In the second place they can't trust you to *play the game*. It's as if your life were a game of Monopoly. You and your friends are all sitting around, the dice comes to you, and you refuse to take your turn. How long are people going to want to play with you if when the dice comes to you, you refuse to take your turn?

EXERCISE #20: INVITE THE TERROR TO TEA

If there is some terrible problem that is frightening and overwhelming, invite it to a mental tea. See what form the problem will take when it opens the door after ringing the bell. A monster, a child, an old man, a beautiful woman, a "thing." Have the monster come into view a little bit at a time. First look at the feet, or maybe there will be shoes, then the body, then the head. Set the table with rare china and silver. Have formal waiters bring delicacies. Tell the problem all your fears, your hatred, your pain. Ask the problem questions. Weep and wail at the problem. Ask the problem what it wants from you. What suggestions it might have. Ask the problem how to solve it. This is a good exercise to bring out our hidden wisdom and insight.

EXERCISE #21: WAITING TO EXHALE

This exercise is for a really bad, black, painful mood. We can imagine that with every breath we breathe out some of the toxic, hard, bitter, gloomy black is being breathed out of our body. And with every breath we breathe in, we are breathing in the white light of healing through the top of our heads. Breathe out the black; breathe in the white healing light. Make the out-breath twice as long as the in-breath. Really force the breath out to the last ounce. Then give yet another push out. When you deplete the lungs this way, the in-breath is easy. Even when you have had trouble breathing due to stress. It's as if the very body is opening up and reaching out for life again.

We can imagine filling up our whole body with the light of healing, letting the white light comfort go to every part of us from the top of our head to the tips of our fingers, down from the top of our head to the tips of our toes. As if, instead of breathing, we *are being breathed* by life itself. Which we probably are.

EXERCISE #22: THE EXERCISE OF EARNESTNESS

Alcatraz is the former prison for hard-core criminals in San Francisco. It was in operation from 1933 until 1963 and it is now a famous-convict museum. The taped interviews of the old inmates are fascinating. Especially after you see their small, pitch-black solitary-confinement cells. It was a problem for the convicts to keep from going "stir crazy." There were no mental health programs. The men knew they were on their own.

Aren't we alone too at three o'clock in the morning, when stress and fear overtake us? We can learn something from these old criminals. How to search within ourselves and find the means to our own salvation through the exercise of earnestness.

Transcendentalist William Channing said, "A man in earnest finds means, or if he cannot find, creates them." 19th-century novelist Bulwer-Lytton said much the same thing, "Earnestness is the best source of mental power." Earnestness is a rare word to hear these days. I think there is power in earnestness, as there is power in decision. Perhaps they are the same.

One convict, who spent a long time in solitary, said that he would tear a button off the top of his pants and flip it in the air. Then, in a place so dark you couldn't see your hand if you waved it in front of you, he would crawl on all fours, like a blind man. He'd feel all around on the floor until he found the button. Then he would stand up and flip the button again. He would do this for hour after hour. He said that's how he kept himself sane.

Another man who was in the total darkness of solitary confinement for a long time said that, with a bit of effort, he would imagine a movie screen appearing against one wall. He would conjure up friends and family upon the screen, and keep up long conversations with them. He would even visit imaginary mountains and beaches that he would visualize on the screen. "You can do it with a little practice," he said, "the colors were always bright and pretty." We must learn to use our mind, or our mind will "use us" to play out its fears, terrors and paranoia in dangerous passive thinking.

Eighteen

Magical-Thinking Exercises

In general, magical thinking should not be used instead of good old-fashioned elbow grease to accomplish the tasks of your life. But magical thinking does have its uses.

Imaginary thinking, including guided imagery, is an indirect way of getting your brain to help you with bodily ills. Nothing happens in the body unless there are messages about it that first pass through the brain. We know the brain is powerful. Magical thinking may be a way we can set the powers of the brain to help us even though we may not know the full extent of those powers. Much can be accomplished with this brain/body, magical-thinking combination.

EXERCISE #1: EMIL COUE'S EVERY DAY
IN EVERY WAY

This is the most famous, most widely used, and probably the very first mind exercise ever devised. Emil Coue was a French pharmacist who introduced to the world a psychotherapy in the 1880s based upon hypnosis. In those days it was called "Suggestion." Coue was the first modern psychologist (Mesmer and Paracelsus were much earlier) to suggest that *our ignorance and weakness* were causing our problems rather than some overwhelming outside force. The solution was to become strong and informed The implication was that anyone could do it.

Emile Coue was the originator of positive self-talk, and would take on a new patient only if he would agree to repeat one phrase over and over to himself as a daily habit, "Every day in every way I'm getting better and better and better."

The mind, *through learned association*, puts these affirmations in touch with the knowledge and experience, already programmed into your memory banks that can help carry them out. The mind is a wonderful servant in this respect. It already has the ball, and can make the touchdown if you point it in the right direction.

Here's the exercise: Say to yourself either out loud or silently, "Every day in every way I'm getting better and better. Every day in every way I'm getting better and better." Keep at it for two minutes, five minutes. As long as it takes. It is not a waste of time. What is a waste of time is thinking I am so stressed out and worried, I'm so depressed. In the case of a skin condition: "Every day in every way my face is becoming clearer and clearer." In the case of a messy house: "Every day in every way the house is becoming neater and neater." In the case of forgetfulness: "Every day in every way my memory is getting better and better," etc.

Once we have taken the edge off the pain of depression with Brainswitching, we can follow that up with this slightly different Directed Thinking technique. We can choose thought patterns which set the brain to working on the actual problem, if only symbolically. Working on the problem, "magically," points the mind in the right direction to subsequently find more realistic solutions.

EXERCISE #2: IMAGINE A HELPER

Many a famous author sits down to write with Dickens or Shakespeare looking over their shoulder as a spirit mentor. We can imagine anybody we want to help us with our daily work, or to find something we are looking for. For instance, I have a whole troop of very tiny imaginary hair fairies, dressed in palest pink with iridescent humming bird wings, that I call upon to "please do your magic and make this mess turn out all right."

This sounds a little cavalier and breezy, I know. But believe me, when I am asking for help I am coming from a very humble and penitent place. Somehow, just the act of opening ourselves up to receive whatever help may be coming our way is a positive psychological exercise that calms the mind.

Since I have been employing them, I notice my hair looks much better than it used to. But more importantly, instead of worrying about my hair, and stressing my subcortex, I use my neocortex to conjure up the fairies. The more details you put into your imaginary helpers the better. Two shades of purple are better than one. The more elaborate the visualization, the more the neurons fire up in your neocortex. And the less the neural activity will be sparking up in your subcortex.

EXERCISE #3: HANG IT ON A HICKORY LIMB

Here's the magical thinking that helps get rid of face blemishes, bad habits, terrible thoughts. Imagine a tree far away, and standing all by itself in a large empty field. It is a magic tree that attracts all the things you want to get rid of: zits, bad habits and painful thoughts. You can send them to this tree. Visualize them fading from your skin, leaving your mind and flying away to the tree which attracts and holds onto them like a super magnet.

EXERCISE #4: ASK-FOR-HELP

We can ask for help at any moment we feel terribly alone. Doesn't matter from whom, or, I found out by experience, from what. It is human nature to become confused and upset over what shores our prior decisions have washed us up on. Surely, we can't have been totally abandoned in this life without recourse to whomever or whatever left us here, and we can ask for help.

One time, in a moment of desperation, after I had gone for a walk in the park to clear my head, I asked help from a tree. It didn't answer me of course, but I immediately felt less alone. There is a sacred presence in every living thing, even a rock. In some way we are connected to everything else. Sometimes just going outside and looking up at the moon, or the stars, can give us a feeling of universal oneness.

At times it is helpful to be specific, like the hair fairies, and ask for help with some particular problem in mind. Other times you can just ask for non-specific help out of the sheer terror of the nothingness, and helplessness you might be feeling at that moment. Here you are asking help from no particular person or entity. Sometimes we can trust that if we earnestly call out, someone hears us and cares. "Hey I'm feeling a little lost here. Could somebody please help me out?" This is magical thinking, to be sure. But it is cognitive thinking, nevertheless. And once you give your brain a problem to solve, you start it moving in a helpful direction, away from stress and anxiety.

EXERCISE #5: A TREE GROWS IN BROOKLYN

Imagine yourself to be a tree. Are you tall, wide, leafy, or bare? Do you have flowers? How are your roots, solid, shallow? If you think your tree is lacking anything, simply re-grow it in your imagination to provide what may be missing, or to make the tree healthier in some way.

EXERCISE #6: TIME BOXES

Time boxes are a wonderful way to set aside problems and give us a little space of calm to rest from our anxious worry.

We can put a worry in a box, and lock it up. Put a sign on it, "Do not open for one hour." When we find out we succeed in delaying our worries for even a short space of time, we start to feel more in control of our thinking. We can say to ourselves, "Okay, I know I have to worry about that. But I'm not going to worry about it right now. I'm going to set it aside. I'm going to wait an hour. Then I'll worry about it."

EXERCISE #7: MAGIC WAND

When my children were young I would sometimes get panicky feelings about their safety at home when my husband and I were at a party, or out to dinner. There was nothing practical I could do about my fear, so I would change my thoughts of worry about them for thoughts of a powerful force field I was erecting around them to protect them. I had a little song that I sang to myself: "I draw a circle around my child to keep them safe from dangers wild." Our imagination, instead of causing us pain by negative imaging of what might possibly go wrong, can go into creating images of something positive and comforting instead. Fear is imaginary anyway, isn't it? If you're going to imagine, imagine the positive. Who knows, in the cosmic scheme of things, the protective field might even work.

EXERCISE #8: INVEST YOUR FEAR

I was over my budget once in remodeling my house. Every time the contractor told me about some added expense my heart froze. I began to feel more and more stressed and anxious as I waited each day for the bad news.

Then I got the idea of turning the fear around. I told myself that for every dollar I spent in remodeling I would receive two dollars profit when I put the house up for sale; which was going to happen shortly as my husband had been transferred to a new office before we were half-way through the house improvements.

The next time the contractor upped some item on me, I thought "Good, I'll make another $150." Yes, this is pure fantasy, magical thinking. But since we don't know what's in the future, why not fantasize something good instead of fantasizing something bad. Most fears never come to pass either, but by the time we know that, the fear has already done our body a lot of harm. By the way, we did make an unlooked for profit on the house as the market suddenly took an upturn.

Nineteen

Self-Awareness Exercises

Self-inquiry exercises help you get in touch with yourself in an existential way. Do you want to know your "real self?" You may be surprised to encounter the self within yourself. Some of these exercises work wonderfully for groups as well.

EXERCISE #1: I AM NOT MY PAIN

I do think there is such a thing as right conduct and that it takes precedence over depression in an educated mind. The trick is, of course, to see that depression is essentially conduct. What helps to make this clear is to learn, from making a constant comparison, the distinction between the "I" and the "Not I". The "I" and the "Not I" exist on either side of the word "am." The difference is that the "Not I" is anything you say *after* you say I am, such as "I am depressed."

We can make use of the "Not I" but we cannot make use of the "I". The only thing we can do with the "I" is *be* it.

However, with depression, the cosmically inert "Not I" seems to be in charge. This is a trick of the human psychological defense system. The source of all our power is the "I." In any earnest confrontation, the "Not I" must ultimately give way to the "I."

Don't try to do this exercise for the first time when you are deep into the pain of depression. It is better to do this exercise, and get the feel of it when you are *not* under great stress. Then, once you have done the exercise and gotten the intellectual idea of it, you can try it out under stress if you want to. But other exercises are better to combat and wrest yourself away from stress and depression

This is not a first-aid exercise

This one is too subtle when you are in terrible anguish. This is not a first-aid exercise. This is an existential exercise to increase your awareness of your awareness. Now, having said that I also want to say that this is the most powerful transcendental exercise there is. It is so powerful that you don't even have to do it. It is the only exercise I know that does itself.

What I mean is that once you have barely read the exercise it immediately penetrates your mind and begins to subtly work as an alarm for your awareness from the first moment. Once you have read this exercise you will never be the same. You will have begun on some level, even if you can't quite get to it yet, to transcend your over-identification with your feelings. The exercise can be expanded to other things besides feelings. And you can make up your own variations.

Here is the exercise: Say to yourself: "I am not my pain. I am the observer of my pain."

Or: "I am not my stress. I am the observer of my stress."

This exercise will help us encounter depression (or stress) in a conscious way. We can begin to separate the defense mechanism of depression from our *will*. It will help distinguish between the physical and the psychological phenomenon of depression, and allow us to choose a more productive behavioral response to it. As we are not our broken arm, neither are we our depression.

Our culture seems to encourage us to identify with depression. How quick we are to do that, and how slow we are to identify with our more positive aspects. For years we work, we create, we travel, and we still don't feel comfortable identifying ourselves as "the artist," "the lawyer," "the musician," "the salesman," the student," or "the writer." We take ourselves to psychiatrists to search for our "authentic identity," our "core self," our "true self."

But let depression hit and whammo, we immediately become *"the depressed."* We self-identify with our pain, and the enmeshment is complete. This exercise helps to create some distance between our depression and our self.

Here are some other variations of this exercise.

I am not worried. I am the observer of my worrying.
I am not happy. I am the observer of my happiness.
I am not stressed. I am the observer of my stress.
I am not angry. I am the observer of my anger.

I am not jealous. I am the observer of my jealousy.
I am not the thinker. I am the observer of my thinking.
I am not wise. I am the observer of my wisdom.
I am not a writer. I am the observer of my writing.
I am not rich. I am the observer of my wealth.
I am not the experiencer. I am the observer of my experience.

EXERCISE #2: WE ARE NOT OUR FEELINGS

It's easier to do exercises that help us recognize that we are not our *pleasant* feelings, rather than to start with exercises to get us to see we are not our negative and depressed feelings. We are more objective about pleasant feelings because most of us are rather tentative about our good feelings and thoughts. We never quite trust them as solid—as if the happy stuff is likely to leave us and disappear at any moment.

There is some validity to this. The recurring thoughts that we are going to lose our happiness sooner than we want—being fearful thoughts themselves—do, sooner or later, bring on bad feelings. Happiness is often temporary because the fearful thoughts that it won't last constitute a self-fulfilling prophecy as they turn into anxious feelings.

We have quite the opposite fear with bad feelings. We see ourselves as set permanently in the cement of our painful feelings or thoughts, and we believe we need outside help to set us free. This time the fear is that the feelings and thoughts will *not* go away, and we are going to feel bad forever.

These fearful thoughts keep engendering more bad feelings. Again, the fear comes true. That's why clinging to happiness out of fear doesn't work, and anxiously wanting painful feelings to end doesn't work. Now if we could *want* our painful feelings to last and *try* to keep them they would disappear as fast as good feelings. But that is another exercise.

This exercise puts some distance between us and our feelings. We can separate out our senses, as we are experiencing them, from our essential selves. This is similar to separating the "I" from the "not I" in exercise #1 above. It is easiest of all to see that we are not our senses, although it is entirely through our senses that we experience the physical world.

Here's the exercise: If we hear a bird singing, we can change the focus on our auditory experience to the observation that *bird song is happening.* If we see a beautiful cloud we can change the focus from our experience of sight to observe that *clouds are happening.* If we are very thirsty and are just ready to down a big glass of water, we can observe that *thirst is being satisfied.*

Then when we get pretty good at this, we can start with the negative stuff. Anger is happening, sadness is happening, fear is happening, instead of the usual "I am angry," "I am sad," or "I am afraid."

EXERCISE #3: A FEELING OF RELIEF

Some people have trouble perceiving their more subtle emotions. Relief is one of them. Do some small hated chore and when you have finished you will have a spark of relief. Of course some people have been in denial for years that they are afraid. These people don't even know what fear feels like. I usually suggest that people take a Toastmasters International Speaking Course if they want to get in touch with their fear. These helpful groups are in every city and very inexpensive. For those who have never done it before, public speaking can be terrifying.

EXERCISE #4: SILENT AS A STONE

We forget the power in silence, and the nourishment. How the mind hates silence. The mind wants to always be busy, and feel important. For ten minutes become a stone. Close your eyes, let your cells start to cement, let the molecules in the body slow down, let the world slow down. Let moss start to grow on top. Let yourself sink onto the earth. Heavy. Silent, No hurry. Waiting. Honorable.

EXERCISE #5: I AM NOW

We get very caught up in who we think we are, and what we have got, and what we have lost, and what we hope for, and who did us wrong, and whom we failed, and what we fear will happen, and what we hate that has already happened.

We get discouraged, bitter, ugly, defensive. Our hearts harden as they fill up with stress. We ride life going ninety miles an hour, and yet we see we never really make any essential progress. We sense that we're still stuck on some ill-fated cosmic see-saw of winning or losing. We go up, down, up, down. Is that all there is?

Life may be more than what we know of it. I used to think maybe life was by the minute. Now I think that maybe life is more by the split second. Only now. Quick now. At the very least this following exercise is a comforting one. It may not make us a winner, but it will make us easier and kinder about whatever it is we think we are losing.

Here is the exercise: We can say to ourselves, I am nobody, really. I don't have any future. I don't have any past. I have been nowhere. I am going nowhere. I am just now.

EXERCISE #6: WITNESS FOR THE PERSECUTION

A powerful exercise for painful feelings, or painful thoughts, is simply to observe them. Feelings are caused by autonomic thinking (self-talk) which may, or may not, be beneath our level of awareness. When we decide, as an act of will, to observe painful feelings as an unconcerned and disinterested witness to them, the neutral, cognitive observation of feelings overrides and replaces the emotional content. The only trick here is to insist that our thinking is simply observation with no judgment, as if the feelings are happening to another person.

Here's the exercise: We simply become a casual bystander to our feelings. "Oh my, here comes another wave of pain," in the same sense that we would comment on ocean wave breaking upon the shore. A casual observer of anything is usually very accepting. There is a difference in accepting our feelings and just feeling them.

EXERCISE #7: CASTING A SHADOW OF SELF

It is good to observe our habitual *emotional* postures just like we study our habitual *thinking* postures. Try to catch sight of yourself in the mirror, or your shadow on the wall. Are you standing up straight and tall, or all hunched over? Are your shoulders back and proud, or are your shoulders hunched over and your chest caved in as if your heart has been grievously wounded as a child? Our best friends are not going to tell us that we often look like "a whipped dog" or "a snarling one," if they want to *remain* our best friends. If you see that your physical posture shows repressed fear, it is time to get in touch with it. (See Exercise #27.)

EXERCISE #8: COMMUNE WITH OUR NATURE

It is always a powerful exercise to be a witness to our thoughts. At first, if we are feeling bad, it will be discouraging, because it will all seem like nothing but garbage is going on. But as we keep looking, deeper and deeper, we will learn a great deal about how our autonomic mind works. Again, the trick is to acknowledge our thoughts without making any judgment upon them. No thoughts of, "I shouldn't be thinking that," or "What a beautiful thought I am thinking."

Just look at the thoughts as they come down the road of your mind. As if they are a line of people passing by your reviewing stand. Oh, yes, a redhead. Look, there's a tall one.

EXERCISE #9: SIT THERE, DON'T JUST DO SOMETHING

This may be the shortest exercise in the world. It takes only one second. To rescue some of our life from the autopilot state, from the unconscious oblivion state, we need to get into the habit of observation, or as the mystic George Gurdjieff has called it, "self-remembering."

We can do this exercise whenever we think about it: Whatever we are doing: walking, buying something in a store, working, talking on the phone, complaining, arguing, suffering, whatever it is, we just STOP. Stop completely, as if we were a car at a stop sign. We are silent. We do not move. We might do the Two Second Shoulder Drop. For one second we just stop and let everything, even our mind, go right on without us while we simply notice that we are here, we are present, we are existing at this place, at this time. We are a witness to this reality; we honor this single moment of our physical incarnation in this life.

It is so sudden a stop that the mind will not be able to come up with another thought so quickly. This exercise helps us see how slow the mind is compared to present reality, how uninterested the mind is in present reality. We just have to tug on our own sleeve, now and then, and come to a complete one-second STOP. After doing this exercise for a while, we will become more alert, more aware. Our whole energy can change. Other people may even start to tell us that our energy is becoming more awake, more alive. And we will start to see that this one-second stop is not really one-second. It is timeless. It is really nothing less than eternity.

EXERCISE #10: THE CENTER WILL HOLD

Sit in a quiet place where you will not be disturbed for twenty minutes. Close your eyes. Relax. Find the very center of yourself. When you get distracted, keep going back to yourself. Some people have described their center as a kind of sunrise of the heart. However you experience the center, go there. It is also the center of the universe. Sometimes you don't have to go anywhere to get where you're supposed to be.

EXERCISE #11: WHAT'S IN A NAME?

Make your name into a stage script by saying it with different emotions. Be sad, pleading, angry, consoling, confiding, chummy, etc. Which emotions are the most comfortable for you? Which emotions are hard to express?

EXERCISE #12: WHAT'S IN A NAME? II

Write your name backwards and then write down the first description that comes to you, don't edit. My name, Arline, spelled backwards is Enilra. My first thought was "fairy elf with wings." Probably some left-over influence from reading *The Lord of the Rings.*

EXERCISE #13: YOU ARE THE OBJECT OF YOUR EYE

Choose some object in the room to represent yourself. And then quickly describe yourself in terms of the object. Write the ideas down quickly, just what comes to you off the top of your head. Is it a book? (I am full of words but I don't talk much). TV? (I'm dramatic). Teapot? (I have something to offer others.) Think about how the object represents you. We can always learn something from ourselves, about ourselves, in this kind of playful exercise.

EXERCISE #14: BECOME AN ANIMAL

This is a write-it-down-quickly kind of exercise. If you were an animal, what kind would you be? Would you be in a forest, in a cage? Quickly choose an animal that you think resembles you in some facet of your being. Describe the animal. Have the animal say something about its life. Then close your eyes and fix in your imagination anything that would make your animal healthier or in a better place. Thank your animal. Open your eyes.

EXERCISE #15: THE BLIND LEADING THE BLIND

Here's another exercise that can help us experience the concept of present reality which is significantly different from what we usually imagine it to be. For this exercise we will need another person to help us. It is an odd exercise so we should get someone who is into this kind of adventurous thinking. This exercise is a bit frightening, so you have to really trust the person to do it carefully.

Here's the exercise: Go to some road that has periodic traffic, not a super highway where cars and trucks are whizzing by constantly. Some country road is best where there may be a minute or two with no car or truck passing. Let your friend blindfold you. Now taking your friend's hand, or holding onto your friend's arm take a walk along the side of the road. Remain at a safe distance but the blindfolded person is on the inside, closest to traffic. The helper is on the outside, away from traffic. The first time a car passes you, or a huge truck, and you are blindfolded, you will be experiencing present reality. You will also be terrified. Your mind will scream with fear. You will think you are going to be run over. But every neuron in your body will be alert, awake and immediately registering the cosmos through your five senses. You can't really judge distance yet because this is a new experience for your mind. You may even rip the blindfold off and leap out of the way. This is okay, part of the exercise.

Then the calculator mind clicks in

The first couple of times a car or truck passes will be an exhilarating, if terrifying, experience of present reality. I guess a roller coaster might provide the same thing. But the roadside exercise is less visceral and more psychological than the roller coaster ride. As you experience the second or third car passing, you will be less afraid, more trusting that you are not going to be hit. Your mind has already, from the first car passing, begun to calculate and anticipate the amount of noise, wind gusts and vibrations that will be occurring, and it will be more and more confident that nothing dangerous is happening.

After a half dozen or so cars pass, your mind will have figured out that even with all the noise, wind and vibrations, you are perfectly okay. The fear will go way down. The mind will have learned "car passing." Now the experience will be more and more taken over by your mind with its instant calculations, its knowing what is going to happen. Less and less will you have the same experience of present reality.

Now you will automatically be switched out of present reality over to the memory banks of your mind. But this is such a powerful experience that you will retain some flavor of the difference between a raw, real, present-reality experience before your mind can steal it from you and substitute its memory tapes for the actual.

EXERCISE #16: THE CAT COMES BACK

Another way to get in touch with hidden fears or hidden motivations is with dramatic play. It works for adults as well as children. Best to do this in a room where we have some space in the middle and won't bump into something. We become a cat. We get down on all fours, close our eyes, arch our back, stretch, let our cells start to change into cat cells, let our eyes start to see as cat's eyes, be the ancient returning of our soul to cat body, act out our feelings, bounce, or pounce, or stalk, or writhe. Twenty minutes is a good time. We can do this to African drum beats too.

EXERCISE #17: THE HEADLESS HORSEMAN

When the white man first came to North America, the Indians thought the white men were crazy because "they thought with their heads and not with their hearts." Somewhere there must have been a mutation that made this difference in people, the difference of relating to the physical world from the feeling area of our hearts, or from the thinking area of our heads. Some small divergence probably appeared at the time the upper brain evolved to join the more primal lower brain.

This is the exercise: It gives an interesting perspective to imagine that we are headless. Just to go through the day without our head. See how we relate to the sky, to the trees, to people with just our heart. We have to relate first, without any thinking strategies about how to do it, or what will work. We will just be responsive to the totality of the messages, rather than sorting them out as to which ones we are going to pay attention to.

Notice that there will not be any quick dismissal or negativity because the heart simply is not capable of negativity. Only the head is capable of negativity as a result of our mind being basically a defense mechanism. The head separates us out from the world so that we can individuate and make distinctions between one thing and another. The heart is not a defense mechanism. It is always receptive, it makes no distinctions between one thing and another. It is our real connection to the world where we can be at one with it. The head speaks and decides. The heart listens and knows.

EXERCISE #18: KEEP YOUR EYE ON THE APPLE

Whenever we start to eat an apple or an orange, we can try to be aware of each cut or each piece as we eat it. Notice, when we start to eat an apple or an orange, how we really enjoy the first bite, "Wow, it tastes good." But after the first bite our attention starts to lapse. After the first bite or two, we can eat the whole apple or orange and not be aware of it at all.

Unless we learn the art of observing ourselves, we kind of fall asleep to 90 percent of our life's experience. Notice how hard it is to observe how we cut up the *whole* apple. We kind of check out after the first slice and the cutting continues by automatic pilot.

We listen to a favorite record, for the first few notes maybe, then it kind of goes on without us. When we start to see this we can get some idea of how odd it is that depression and anxiety don't just go on without us too. We get some idea that maybe we are hanging on to them unwittingly. We may start to wonder how we hang on to every nuance of anxiety, stress, and depression, but not hang on to half the notes of a favorite song.

EXERCISE #19: THE ART OF SILENCE

Most of us have very little of silence about us. Even when we are not talking, our thoughts are screaming bolts of energy racing through our minds. We are enduring slights, we are smarting from injustices, we are celebrating small victories and agonizing over small failures. We are contemplating our illnesses. We are planning small revenges, and plotting quick retreats.

We are a whirl of psychic road maps, loves, hates, wants, needs, dreams, fears, annoyances all vying for our attention at the same time. No wonder when we sit down with one another, we feel alienated and not close. Remember the law of physics—that every action has an equal and opposite reaction? Our thoughts are bio-electrical. They exist as physical realities. Our minds are yelling at each other.

Here's the exercise: We could start to get some distance from all these agitating thoughts. We could begin to free our subjugation to our thoughts and feelings by deciding to sit quietly for one hour at the same time every day, and getting used to seeing how frantic our mind is. Since we are not our mind, *we* don't have to be frantic. We can choose a time early in the morning before our duties begin, or late at night when others have usually retired.

At first we will think it is a waste of time just watching the mental garbage float by. But just watching, with no judgment, no complaint, pretty soon things will slow down. Thoughts will be less frequent. Just watch as if we were any movie patron sitting in the theater watching the play on the screen. We watch the play going on across the screen of our mind.

Just calm, just silent, nowhere to go, nothing to do. Leave questions unanswered, sentences unfinished. Some people work up to doing this for literally hours. Silence is not just the absence of noise, it is the presence of ourselves.

Something of this silence and calm will go with us during the day. People will begin to experience us as less harsh to be with, less heavy. It will be almost nourishing to others, who sense on some level that when they are next to us they seem to have more space.

EXERCISE 20#: EMPTY *OF* MIND EXERCISE

This exercise is an improvement on the more well-known Empty Your Mind Exercise. **WARNING:** The Empty Your Mind Exercise is often used in various training groups but I don't recommend it. The Empty Your Mind exercise, *instead* of getting us to identify with the *observer* of the mind, mistakenly gets us to identify with *emptiness*. The point of my exercise is to recognize that *we are not our mind*. By observing our mind, even briefly, we can begin to identify with the observer of the mind rather than mind itself.

Now if we are struggling with a lot of garbage in our mind which is torturing us, maybe emptiness provides temporary release, but it does not lead to any kind of transcendental understanding. Release *from* suffering is not the same thing as release *of* suffering. If we must do this exercise, let's do it this way: *We should empty ourselves of our mind*. That works!

Here's the exercise: Sit quietly and imagine the mind as a huge garbage can full of debris–thoughts, images, sounds, colors. Have a garbage truck come by to pick up the garbage. Throw out the thoughts and images into the truck one by one and when it is almost empty, toss in the can. Now where can your thoughts reside with no mind? When one comes along, just hang it over the clothesline far away, and then let the wind come and blow it farther over the hill.

EXERCISE #21: ALICE IN WONDERLAND

In this exercise we imagine we are growing bigger and bigger. At first we are just giants. Then we grow so large we are bigger than the trees and the buildings. In fact, now the trees and the buildings are inside us. We swallow the whole sky up and the clouds are moving inside this vastness that we have become. After a while we are so big that the whole world is in us, instead of the other way around.

There is a comforting feeling that comes with our being so much bigger than life, bigger than the world and its problems. We reach ourselves all the way out. We are absolutely unlimited. Remember that the mind in retrospect cannot tell the difference between an imagined and a real experience. Naturally you will afterward reject this as a real happening, but the mind will register the feelings of "oneness," of "being in charge," "feeling expansive," and "at peace."

EXERCISE #22: LISTEN TO THE MUSIC

Ever wonder why we get tired of a favorite song? Why it doesn't give us the same thrill hearing the hundredth time as it did the first? It's because our mind steals it from us. The minute the mind can understand the music, it gets us to go on auto-pilot, listening to the mind's replay of it the minute the first notes begin.

A good exercise is to force ourselves to listen to the music a new way. Concentrate on the spaces between the notes and this will confuse the mind so that we can enjoy a more present experience again, instead of being whisked by the mind into its lifeless autopilot rendition. The mind can fool us very easily if we are satisfied with hearing the music instead of *becoming the music.*

Or we can make sure we are open to the song from the region of the heart instead of the head. Some songs are written from a head space and these will never make it to the heart space. But music that is written from the heart space can be ruined by letting it come to us head first.

We can just lower our energy like a descending thermometer from the head to the heart and let the space open up to receive the music. Of course there is some music that can resonate lower in the power center of the body— rock-and-roll for instance. Music is an opportunity to get some distance between our thoughts and our feelings. We can leave off collapsing into our mind and collapse into the music instead. That's why music is such a great release. It is a release from the mind.

I have done healing also with heart-space music. If I have the flu, or a twisted knee I imagine that the music is moving to the area of the problem and healing me. (I should remember to do it more often.)

EXERCISE #23: NINETY YEARS OLD AND ON YOUR DEATHBED

"What have I lived for?" These were the last words of Moss Hart, of the famed duo Rogers and Hart, whose Broadway musicals were legend. Perhaps at the end of our life we may all ask the same question. And have no answer. But the exercise does get us to view our lives more objectively. We may see something we otherwise might have missed.

I read about a woman who told her psychiatrist that, except for the profoundly retarded son for whom she was solely responsible, there was nothing else in her life. She said that the child, who could neither speak nor understand her, and who needed constant care, could likely live another forty years, when she herself would be ninety.

"So," said the psychiatrist, "If all you did for the rest of your life was take care of this child, provide him comfort and companionship and love, would you consider that you had wasted your life?"

The woman thought for a minute and then responded, *as if she realized it for the very first time.* "No, I guess not. I think if all I did was care for my child, and give him comfort and love until he dies, that my life would not have been wasted."

Here's the exercise: Imagine you are getting ready to die. Imagine yourself laid out on a bed of crisp white sheets in a plain room with white walls and hazy windows. You are very still, arms and legs stretched out and motionless. There is nothing moving about in the room to distract you. You are completely alone. There is utter silence in the room. You are very old. You have only a few minutes of life left now. What is really important to you now, now that you have to leave it all behind anyway? What about all the worries and fears that you spent so much time with? Are you going to take those with you when you die, or leave them behind? How important are they, these worries, fears and regrets, now that you are going to die?

EXERCISE #24: CONSCIOUS CUP OF TEA

A dead person cannot enjoy a cup of tea. But sometimes when we are drinking a cup of tea, if we are just on automatic pilot, how alive are we? How alive or dead to our senses have we become as we are rushing heedlessly about our daily humdrums?

We could stop for five minutes and have a conscious cup of tea. We could notice how the cup feels warm and comforting in our hand. We could breathe in the aroma as it wafts upward, hear the sound of the cup as we set it down on the table or desk. We could open ourselves up and make space for the whole taste and pleasure of it.

Our mind is not at all interested in a conscious cup of tea. Our mind has long ago decided that it has "done tea" already, and at the first sip wants to slip us into auto-pilot tea. When you can take your tea drinking back from the mind, you start to see how you are not your mind.

EXERCISE #25: THE WORLD IS A DREAM, WHAT PART OF YOU IS THEM?

This is another good exercise for getting practice in observing our habitual emotional mindsets. Psychiatrists have helped us get a handle on our hidden motivations and fears through the process of dream analysis. Our dreams may be frightening or confused, but we can understand that it is we, ourselves, who people our dreams with thoughts and feelings that take the roles of people, things and events.

At first we may be shocked when we tell the therapist about some mean act perpetrated upon us in our dreams by a hated rival and hear the question, "Okay, now *what part of you* does this person symbolize?" We can get pretty good at seeing that even the worst monsters in our nightmares are *really aspects of our own motivations or fears.*

One way to describe the human experience is to say that our physical circumstances are always, in some profound way, the reflection of some part of our essential selves. We are never wrong if we assume that whatever is happening to us is the physical reflection of our inner being. It gives us the essential clue *that to change the outside circumstances of our lives, if we wish to do so, we must change ourselves from within.*

Here's the exercise: We can analyze our daily life as if it were a dream we had last night. What part of us is being reflected in "them." What part of us is reflected in the belligerent neighbor who is arguing over the property line. What part of us is symbolized in the insult our spouse just tossed our way.

Here's a hint: anger is fear turned out, weakness is fear turned in. This is another way of widening our horizon and becoming more objective about what life seems to be throwing at us, so that we might not become lost in our troubles but, instead, be able to transcend them.

EXERCISE #26: ANGER IS FEAR AND GREAT ANGER IS GREAT FEAR

At our very core we hate what we fear. This makes perfect sense because this mechanism, fear, was the only thing we had in our early stages of development to allow us to survive a hostile environment. As a caveman, our operation was pretty simple: There is danger: fear arises, and we strike or run.

With the continuing development of our higher cognitive faculties, other possibilities have emerged between the fear and the strike or run. Now it is not always practical, legal, moral or ethical to go the simple route. It could result in road rage, or Little League Lunacy.

Our fears are complex and subtle. The line from fear to strike or run is murky. Instead of stark fear being necessary to keep us from danger, over the eons of our social advances we've developed dislike and avoidance techniques. In a complicated system, like the human being, little things can go wrong. When our fear can't end up in some action for our benefit, we do not usually know what to do with the unused fear. It hangs in our body and makes us depressed and hostile. We're mean to our nearest and dearest. We get angry. We start to hate everybody.

Here's the exercise: If we are really angry, it might help to remember that anger is fear and great anger is great fear. We need to save ourselves from our fear more than we need to save ourselves from any enemy. The way we save ourselves from our fear is simply to feel it while accepting it. It won't kill us.

EXERCISE #27: GETTING IN TOUCH WITH YOUR FEAR

We are much too afraid of our fear. If we were as afraid of our backyard weeds as we are of our fear, we would avoid and ignore our weeds, we would decide not to think about our weeds, not do anything to keep them under control and our yard would soon engulf us like a jungle

When we want to get in touch with our fear, we won't have to search long. We have little fears all the time that we've learned to avoid. Now we can pay attention to them. One of the first fears I discovered was a fear to make phone calls if I was expecting some disappointment or had to tell someone something difficult for them to hear. I started to realize that I put off difficult phone calls until "later," or I would forget to call at all, or I would misplace the number. It was less painful to blame non-calling on being lazy, or disorganized, or forgetful than face the fact I was afraid. I knew how to deal with laziness, or disorganization, or forgetfulness. I hadn't the slightest idea what to do about my fear.

When I got user-friendly with my fear, going out of my way to confront it instead of avoiding it, I began to see how little power it had. My fear was just a big dog with menacing fangs and a big bark that whimpers and cowers when you face it down. Today when I think about difficult calls, I feel the fear buzz inside my chest, like a little electric shock. I carry that fear buzz right to the phone and make the darn calls.

Blame and fear

Another way to encounter our repressed fear is anytime we find ourselves blaming anyone or anything. Change the focus from the object of our blame to ourselves and try and feel any feelings we might be having at that instant.

One clue is that fear HURTS! Even a little fear can buzz around the heart, or stomach, or throat. Breathing will be more shallow. I still have fear, but I've developed a different relationship to it. It is now invited and accepted rather than ignored. I welcomed my fear back into my daily life. It's no more to me than a roller coaster ride. I was scared to death. WHEW! That was a good one!"

Another way to get in touch with repressed fear is in things we "hate" to do. Hate is just fear projected outward onto something or someone. For instance, I don't mind filling the dishwasher, but I "hate" emptying it. When I focus awareness on any fear that might be going on by taking the focus off how I hate to empty the dishwasher. I always catch that tiny electric buzz, or at least some shallow breathing, the tight throat, or tense shoulders. Awareness has elevated emptying the dishwasher to a higher experience. Once in touch with little fears, we can tackle bigger ones. The more we practice this, the more we'll know what to practice.

When you accept your fear you then become free from your fear. (Remember there is a difference in feeling fear and accepting the feeling of fear). Once accepted by you, your fear can no longer be the hidden factor in your relationship to the world.

Fear and Immaturity

I have come to the conclusion that it is this hidden fear that keeps people in a constant state of suspended immaturity. For years I had been trying to figure out what is the reason that some people don't seem to "catch on" to life. They don't get a good education or a good job. They are not great socially; they either talk too much or not enough They are quick to blame others for any perceived lack—the government, society, the rich, corporate greed, bigots, racists, the "big people" as opposed to them, the self-perceived "Lesser People." etc., etc.

I was trying to figure out what was the missing ingredient in their thinking. I figured early on that it was *not* self esteem. But what was it? What precept would enable them to get a jumpstart, to finally see life as the rest of us see life? I finally concluded that it was old repressed fear that held them back from risking themselves in the normal learning experiences of life.

Risk is always daunting

We all find risk difficult due to the normal fear associated with any new endeavor. These lesser-functioning people are not just dealing with "current fear." They have never addressed their childhood terror (whatever it was—a mother who screamed at them, alcoholic father who got drunk and punitive, bullies at school or older siblings who teased them unmercifully or sexual abused them).

So they are way behind their peers in the practical experience of developmental milestones—making friends the first day at school, first dance, first stab at approaching a girl, or a guy for a date. Their peers can accomplish these growth events because they can dredge up the normal amount of courage to overcome a normal amount of fear. But for a person with a bunch of repressed fear that they are not even aware of, these situations are not just scary, they are terrifying. They need much more courage than their more normal counterparts. If they *knew* they needed courage, they could probably exercise it. But not knowing their own repressed fear is the issue, instead of calling on their own courage, they focus on the scariness of the situation and decide to "sit it out." No one can be mature and fearful.

EXERCISE #28: NAME THAT FEELING. IS THAT YOUR FINAL ANSWER?

Carrying on a conversation with ourselves forces us to light up some neurons in the neocortex which automatically causes a healthy "brown out" in our emotional subcortex. We have only a finite amount of electricity.

Sometimes our feelings get a chance to dig in and entrench themselves when we are unaware. To balance this we can at any moment call ourselves on what we have going on, feeling-wise. We can say something like: "Oh yes, I recognize this. This is depression," or, "Perhaps there might be a little mania occurring at the moment."

How is this helpful? The worst part about feelings is when we forget they are not us, and we limit ourselves to what we are *feeling* instead of seeing feelings as simply one part of the picture of life, a picture that may be immediately changed because we are the artist, not the canvas.

One of the reasons for the success of suicide hot lines is getting people to talk about their situation. By describing and talking about their feelings, which is cognitive rather than emotional activity, they slowly pull out of being stuck in the clutches of their fear. Once people start the cognitive neurons in motion they can cause a brain shift of activity which will help get them out of the subcortex of painful feelings into the neocortex where painful feelings do not reside.

EXERCISE #29: AUTONOMIC WRITING

Just sitting down and writing whatever comes to our hand is a good way to see what kind of things are going on in our mind that are influencing us in ways we don't realize. We can get in touch with long-held opinions or precepts which we are carrying but of which we may not be totally aware. Set aside a time–ten minutes is enough, an hour is not excessive. Journaling can take us on a fascinating journey into the hidden workings of our thinking and being.

We can write down goals and aspirations, and find that by writing them they become clearer and more possible. We can write down things we are grateful for. We can write down affirmations that help to influence a more positive mindset. There is a connection between our handwriting and our mind. They can influence each other. Even if we are at a total loss as to what to write, we can just write down a list of words, and reading them over, get some idea of where to go next.

A journey of thousand miles starts with a single step. A journal of a thousand pages begins with a single word. Write down one word. Already the second word will be forming.

EXERCISE #30: WHO AM I

Who am I? In five minutes write down as many answers as you can to that question. Keep the paper and do the exercise again at different times. Date and keep the papers for future reference. Read them over from time to time. See how the answers change. I am a doctor, I am a failure, I am a mother, I am sad, I sing, I am wrong, I am sick, I am a child of the universe.

Twenty

Anti-Stress Exercises

Exercises are helpful in changing the kind of self-focused thinking that tends to disconnect us from present reality. It has been proven many times that the simplest one-second exercise can reduce stress. Something as simple as wadding up a piece of paper and pitching it into the wastebasket in a mock basketball throw can break the cement of your tension and give you a space to relax into.

EXERCISE #1: TWO-SECOND SHOULDER DROP AND INSTANT BACK RELEASE

This exercise is wonderful for releasing stress, and it is also valuable for helping us see what kind of things put us under stress that we didn't know put us under stress. Do it dozens of times during the day, whenever you think about it. Stress on the body puts stress on the mind. Stress on the mind causes anxiety leading to a chemical shift that can become depression.

Here's the exercise: Take two seconds out of your busy life. Focus awareness on shoulders and let them drop. Focus awareness on back and let it collapse. Let your upper body collapse forward. Let you head hang forward, loose, loose, one second... two seconds. Check out other areas of tensed muscles, the throat, the tongue, the hands and let them also relax.

I asked a woman who was in therapy for marriage counseling whether she knew, at any particular time, if she were under stress. She answered, "Oh, yes, I'm always under stress *when he.* . ." I stopped her in mid sentence and remarked as kindly as possible that those two words *when he* were very damning evidence that she did not have a very intimate connection to *her own* feelings.

Most people do not have an intimate enough connection with their own body to know whether or not they are under small amounts of stress at any particular moment. They judge their degree of stress, not by the feel of their body, but by the regular context in which full-blown stress appears. They judge their feelings by what is happening in their outside environment: failures, disappointments, bad news, what other people are doing or saying.

People understand, in general, that they have feelings. But specifically they don't really know them *from spark to finish.* We're mostly aware of *full-blown feelings* when they're exacerbated enough to capture our attention by their huge discomfort.

It is common sense to know ahead of time what circumstances will stress us out so that we can prepare for them. But these peak stress periods may not tell enough of the story. We should be able to check in on ourselves in less important moments and see what stress we are building up during the course of a normal day when nothing supposedly stressful is occurring.

If we would check up on ourselves, most of us would see we are winding ourselves up tighter and tighter all day long, like a clock spring, ratcheting up little by little because we don't know we are ratcheting up. Then at the end of the day we have a lot of built-up stress which we have not used up in some kind of action.

Stress not spent in action is stored in your body

Whatever stress is not spent in action, or is not recognized and simply released as stress per se, gets stored in the body and will end up disturbing us in some way. Some people hold their stress in backaches, some in headaches, some in stomach problems. This exercise ratchets down, all during the day what we are ratcheting up.

During our waking hours our body is always under some physical stress from the effects of gravity alone. Without stress we wouldn't be able to build up our muscle strength. Since there is always some tension, we can always effect a small relaxation as an act of will. If we start to do this as a matter of course, dozens of times throughout the day, we will start to notice that our back and shoulders are tighter than we think sometimes. We will start to see that even normal activities cause a build-up of stress.

One time I was doing this exercise during a writer's meeting. I was shocked to learn that listening to other people read their work put me under a lot of stress. I kept releasing my back and releasing my back. I had no idea that this was a stress-provoking activity for me. I had always thought that listening to other people read was a kind of relaxation for me.

This exercise is not only wonderful for releasing stress, it is also wonderful for helping us see what kind of things put us under stress that we didn't know put us under stress.

EXERCISE #2: CRACK THE GREAT STONE FACE

Abraham Lincoln once said that a man was not responsible for the look of his face before he was forty, that it was a quirk of nature. But a face after forty depended upon the man himself and his temperament. One of my grandmother's favorite expressions, when she was criticizing someone for looking sour or disagreeable all the time, was "you'd think a smile would crack his face."

I use the smile exercise every day of my life. I think about it at odd times during my regular activities. It only takes about two seconds. No more. It is a marvelous kind of immediate relaxation that has long-term consequences in promoting over the years a more smooth and pleasant countenance, and mental attitude of positivity. In a way it is a psychological mind *and* face-lift

The idea is that we don't realize how our faces get set in cement-like masks of determination, concentration, anxiety, and judgment. These expressions become etched on our face in the form of wrinkles and furrowed brows, and we have no idea how much stress and strain we are collecting and holding in all these little muscles.

Sometimes we concentrate so hard we look like we are in pain, or angry. Our faces become as tense and frozen as those carved in stone on Mount Rushmore. When our muscles are set like this, our face is in a stress syndrome. When any part of our body is in stress, our mind starts to feel anxious. This exercise will release a great deal of accumulated frustration, negativity, judgment and stubbornness.

Here's the exercise: Say to yourself, "Crack the great stone face," and become aware of any tension in your face. Relax the face and bring it into a slow, easy s-m-i-l-e. At the same time let the shoulders down and relax them as well.

You don't need to fear that if you do this in public people will notice. I caught myself in the mirror one time after I had achieved a "slow smile" and was shocked to find that the smile, which felt wide to me, was barely perceptible in the mirror. But you know what? I'll bet the anxiety in my face *before* the exercise was quite noticeable to any onlooker.

Stress is fear

I did this exercise recently while listening to an acquaintance go into a long harangue about something I thought was way off base. I was getting more and more stressed but wanted to be polite, and accept another point of view. I realized that my opposition to the point was probably showing up in my face because I felt really tense. But once I relaxed my face and did the "slow smile" (I did the exercise while looking intently at the speaker), I found my whole self relaxed and I could be much more accepting of the person even though I thoroughly disapproved of her argument. And we should always remember that any kind of stress is some type of fear.

Sometimes I use this exercise at night just before I go to sleep just to make sure I'm not going to sleep with a frown on my face. It only takes a second or two. If you get in the habit of thinking about this exercise during the day you will be surprised how often you catch yourself being a Great Stone Face. You may even start to laugh at yourself for being SO SERIOUS.

EXERCISE #3: BELLY BREATHING

"Belly breathing" should take care of panic attacks in 15 or 20 minutes. When your symptoms start, recognize that you have been breathing in your upper chest. To stop the scary symptoms (diziness, fear of fainting etc.) you need to change the way you are breathing. You need to move the air down into the belly thus involving the entire lung. To do this, follow these simple instructions.

1. RELAX with the "Shoulder Drop And Back Release" (Exercise. #1)," and "Crack The Great Stone Face" (Exercise #2)
2. Put one hand on your chest, the other on your abdomen.
3. Take a slow, easy breath in thru your nose to the count of five. Make sure your chest stays quiet. Your belly will expand. This way you will involve the whole lung.

4. Hold for the count of five
5. Release air slowly to the count of five. While releasing purse your lips and make a hissing sound. Notice how your belly goes in as you breathe out. How it goes out as you breathe in.

Put all your concentration on the breathing. Repeat this exercise as many times as necessary. It is also helpful to practice this breathing when you are not feeling the symptoms. Set up a plan for yourself. For instance, every time you stop for a red light, or every time the phone rings take a belly breath. Then you will be ready to use this breathing in a panic situation.

If it is hard for you to take a breath, It helps to exaggerate the breathing out–give a long extra puff of exhale to empty out even more air—beyond what you thought was your last bit. When you're this empty you naturally breathe in to fill up.

Concentrate on the breathing itself. Don't concentrate on the worry that you can't breathe. Make a conscious choice between the two things: Worry about breathing or breathing itself. No need to panic anymore over panic attacks. Just breathe. Soon your calmer feelings will reflect the peaceful thoughts about breathing.

EXERCISE #4: WHEN THINGS ARE CLOSING IN, ENLARGE THE HORIZON

When we are struggling with a difficult problem, we rightly tend to focus on our problem. We box it in, contain it, separate it out of the generality of our lives so we can really see it. This is fine, as long as our focus leads to action. But if no action is possible and we are still focused, our focus, instead of ending in action, ends in itself. We end up in the box with the problem, separated from everything else, and wonder why we feel like things are closing in on us. Things aren't closing in; we have allowed a prudent problem-solving mechanism to become an end in itself, instead of a means to an end.

The way out is the same as the way in. We can come out of the box into the generality of our life. If our problem is one of poor health, for instance, we can expand our awareness to include the resources of our family, our accomplishments, our spiritual life. We can expand our awareness in terms of time. We can see the problem, not as a separate time frame of weeks, or months, but as part of an 80-year life-span. We can look at the small wild things in nature, at the grand mountains, or the endless sky and see that no one problem is bigger than life itself. And life is always on our side.

EXERCISE #5: DON'T GIVE 100 PERCENT EFFORT

This is an old Zen exercise. When we are striving for excellence, deep into some lengthy project and feel burn-out starting, it sometimes helps to give only three-fourths effort instead of 100 percent. It is a way of tricking the mind. When we let up the pressure, we find that 25 percent of our effort is being wasted in anxiety and fear of failure, and it is usually this that we give up when we only give 75%.

EXERCISE #6: COLOR ME BLUE, OR PINK, OR POLKA DOT

This exercise is based upon the fundamental principle which makes hypnosis possible: the mind can only entertain one thought at a time, and we can choose any thought we want. It is a good exercise for getting some calm distance from anxious feelings or painful thoughts by developing the knack of being able to observe disturbing feelings without actually succumbing to the compulsion to collapse into them.

Some people use this exercise to get rid of painful feelings and thoughts, and some use it to get rid of headaches. Curing headaches may be a happy byproduct of the exercise. But the real existential value of this exercise is to begin to establish the idea for ourselves that we are essentially more powerful than our feelings, even our feelings of pain. We can learn to manage ourselves in the face of them, rather than allowing the feelings to manage us. It helps if you try this exercise at first when you are only slightly anguished or stressed, or have just a little headache. The exercise is much too complex to use as a quick fix for extreme anxiety.

Here is the exercise: Describe the feelings, or the pain, in great imaginary detail. What color is my headache? How big is it? Where is it located? How painful is it on a scale of one to ten. That feeling of anxiety or fear—where is it located in my body? Is it solid or liquid? What shape is it? Is it moving or standing still?

Neutral thoughts about coloring our headache, or deciding on the shape and position of our bad feeling start to interrupt and can even replace the thought "I am in pain." Because these neutral thoughts require cognitive and verbal effort, as we increase our concentration upon them, they power up the neuronal activity in the neocortex, and power down the neuronal activity in the subcortex.

EXERCISE #7: SPEAKING IN TONGUES

Here is another play-acting exercise. Find a quiet place. Stand up so it is possible to move around and make gestures. Close the eyes. Start talking in gibberish, any syllables—ush, uu, ah, eoeolala— just keep it up for about ten minutes. Put some power and drama into it. Speaking in this non-language talk about your fears, pain, hopes, betrayals. Notice how easy it is to *talk* gibberish but it is not easy to *think* gibberish. Talk is cheap. But it is a good release for pent-up angst.

EXERCISE #8: ON THE BEACH FOR 30 SECONDS

Keep a conch shell on your desk. Listen to the sound of the sea.

EXERCISE #9: SEEK PLACES OF SILENCE

In a busy world it is easy to forget how nourishing silence may be. Where can you go to find it? Visit a small, old, used bookstore. Walk into a church or a graveyard.

EXERCISE #10: PACK UP YOUR TROUBLES

Imagine a worry box. Write down your worries on imaginary paper. Put the paper in the box for safekeeping while you go to sleep.

EXERCISE #11: SLOW DOWN TIME

This exercise is good when you're starting to fill up with a lot of anxious worry about being late. Interrupt the anxious worry in the subcortex by switching to the neocortex and visualize a clock. Move the hands back in time. Or you can visualize the earth turning on its axis and, in your imagination, stop the earth from spinning. With this kind of magical thinking, you will fool the subcortex into thinking "something is being done" about your being late, and your anxiety will lessen. The mind is not as smart as you are. Keep doing the exercise as long as you are agitated. Any kind of neocortical activity is calming to the mind because as long as you are thinking a non-stressful thought, the stressful thought cannot get through to your attention.

EXERCISE #12: THE CHAOS OR SWEEPING DIRT THEORY

This exercise is for perfectionists who feel bad if their life is not in pristine order, or their business is not absolutely running at tip-top efficiency all the time. A poem by Rudyard Kipling begins *"If you can keep your head while all about you are losing theirs and blaming it on you..."* In a way our modern lives are so complicated and seemingly behind the clock that, to survive, you somehow have to become the eye of your own hurricane.

How do you manage such a thing? I think you manage it by becoming philosophical. When you become philosophical you become more objective about things. When you become more objective, you become calmer. You don't expect so much from yourself that it pits you against everybody else in a constant state of competition.

When you think of the universe, you can see that there is some kind of order in all the chaos. We can search for that order in our own chaotic lives. We are all at cross-purposes with life all the time. We're always trying to finish and complete something, and life is always showing us that there will always be something left undone.

We build our houses and from the beginning we can see they slowly slide into disrepair. There's nothing solid that lasts forever, so we shouldn't get so upset if the carpet color didn't turn out right. I like to think of life as sweeping dirt. I have a nice house with wood floors and oriental rugs but I don't always manage to have it all clean and spotless. I am no different from a woman who lives in a hut with a dirt floor. My life is privileged, yes, but I can't hold everything together anymore than she can. I make no essential progress either.

In a way we're all just sweeping dirt so we can make a small, smooth place to sit down and share a cup of tea.

Here's the exercise: When you can't hold it all together, when what you did yesterday needs to be done all over again today, think of all life as having no essential progress, that we're all in the same boat, we're all "just sweeping dirt."

EXERCISE #13: TAKE A WALK ON THE WILD SIDE

When you are stressed, anxious, over-tired and basically stale on life it is probably because you have been confining yourself to four walls somewhere at home or at work. A human being is, first and foremost, an animal. Animals don't do well in cages. Take five minutes out of your schedule and go outside. A natural environment has less stress-provoking stimuli. Look at the sky. Look at the trees. At night look up at the stars. If possible, plan a vacation to the wilderness. Many people find this to be a life-changing experience in that some essential existential loneliness seems comforted.

"The creatures of the wilderness have long been trying to tell us some immense secret that we have not quite heard. Sometimes we get very close. When we are tired and sad, we look up at the glistening stars, and imagine that they might be looking back at us. When we are frightened and lonely, the trees in the park cheer us somehow. We can be running fast on a hard road when suddenly we catch sight of some small wild thing in our path. We stop and look. We rest a moment. We almost understand."(from the children's book *Time of the Wild.*)

EXERCISE #14: LET YOUR WORRIES
GO UP IN SMOKE

Write down a list of worries. Burn the list.

EXERCISE #15: SHOULDA, COULDA, WOULDA

I have no idea why this exercise should work. I only know that it does reduce stress. Perhaps because we aren't fighting our disappointments anymore but making light of them. A lot of anxious worry and guilt concerns our unfinished or untried projects that we are hanging onto. We are not hanging onto them because we are going to do them. We are hanging onto them in order to self-abuse ourselves. Hanging on to them has become an "unconscious" ingrained habit. We need to turn this hidden habit into something more visible so we don't keep tripping ourselves over it.

Whenever we become unhappy with ourselves, jealous of others, sad about our failure we can just say, "Oh, everybody has shoulda, woulda, coulda. Shoulda, woulda, coulda. Shoulda, woulda, coulda." Say it over and over for about 30 seconds. Make it kind of a song. After doing this a while, you will be able to quickly substitute this short 30-second light-hearted exercise for the much longer, much more painful anxious worry that goes on and on. Interrupt the ingrained worry with the short-cut worry and finish early.

EXERCISE #16: JUST DON'T DO IT!

Write a list of all you plan to do for the day. Drop one item from your list.

EXERCISE #17: ADOPT-A-HIGHWAY-CLEAN-UP AT HOME

Our environment should be nurturing instead of stealing energy from us. A highway is pleasant and relaxing to drive when it is clean, and unpleasant and stressful when it is littered with trash. Our homes are unpleasant and stressful when they are cluttered with a pile-up of things which could be put away or thrown away. Highways and homes get messy the same way—*one piece at a time*. We are all busy. We may not have even five minutes to clean up. But we always have five seconds as we are walking by.

Every time we walk through a messy room, we can reach out our hand to put one thing away, or throw one thing away. Put the milk back in the refrigerator. Hang up one towel. Hang up one shirt. Throw away one piece of newspaper. Put one dirty dish in the dishwasher. Clean one foot of kitchen counter space. Cumulative problems can be overturned by cumulative effort. Cumulative result has been working against us. We can put cumulative effort to work *for* us, and watch our home or our car get magically neat the same effortless and inevitable way it got messy.

EXERCISE #18: ANY PLAN IS
BETTER THAN NO PLAN

Any plan of action is better than no plan. Just having a plan is sometimes half the job right there. As Benjamin Franklin said, "Well begun is half done."

When my children were little, the house would get into a terrible mess when all five of them were home. I found that any plan to pick up was better than no plan. I had a couple of plans.

One plan I called LPC Pickup. I would call everybody together and make an announcement, "Okay, you guys, LPC in the Living Room and the number is 20." This meant that each child had to pick up and throw away 20 small pieces of stuff (LPC: Little Pieces of Crap) in the Living Room. A piece of broken Christmas ornament, a piece of tinsel, a small scrap of paper. Anything counted so you can be sure some of the debris picked up was practically microscopic just to be ornery. But 100 pieces picked up in less than a minute can make a huge difference. And it was often quicker and easier to pick up big things than little things anyway.

Another plan was called ABC Pickup. Each child was to get as far through the alphabet as possible by picking up or putting away something that started with A (ads in a newspaper, apple core, air–there's always a joker in the crowd) B (books, although some books qualified for the A category or other categories), C (clothes), etc. There is some mystical power to any plan.

EXERCISE #19: JUST WHITTLE IT DOWN

This is very similar to the exercise above it. But this refers not just to cleaning up, but to accomplishing any large project or build-up of accumulated tasks to be done which seem overwhelming when you think about all of it. Turn your attention from the whole task and just do any one small thing that takes you closer to the finish line. You can say to yourself, "I just have to keep whittling it down, whittling it down."

EXERCISE # 20: CONSCIOUS WORRY

The most dangerous thing about worry is that you are seldom aware you are doing it until you are so deep you can't stop. The reason you can't stop is that it's hard to stop doing something, as an act of will, that you have been doing automatically for so long. The worrying habit is especially hard.

One way to help break the worry habit is to transfer some particular long-standing worry from "auto-pilot" status to "on-purpose" status. Things that you habitually do "on purpose" are easier to *stop doing* on purpose. Plan a 30-second worry about some particular problem. Worry. Worry. Worry. Now stop worrying. You can do this 30-second exercise all during the day, whenever you start to worry about something.

There is another kind of worry which is not non-specific. We get anxious and worried about nothing in particular. This is also a habit. Plan to worry, in general, for 30 seconds.

Now stop. If you wish, you can reschedule more worry at a later time which should give you some peace between now and then.

EXERCISE #21: UNFOCUS ON STRESS

Look up from your work. Let your eyes go unfocused, then gaze lazily into the distance. Do this for 10 seconds.

Then do the "Shoulder Drop And Back Release" (Exercise #1)," and "Crack The Great Stone Face" (Exercise #2)

EXERCISE #22: NOW YOU SEE IT, NOW YOU DON'T

The mind is a great computer. If we use it wisely we can avoid a lot of stress, and add some efficiency to almost any area of our life. Sometimes work piles up—housework, office work, projects. When we are rushing to and fro we get hit with the thought of a bill we haven't paid, a report that's overdue, or we notice the dust on the lamp table in the living room.

One way we can use these noticings is to horrible-ize them. I'll never get the money to stretch this month. And there's a bigger report due next week, and then the yearly final. The whole house needs a good cleaning and I don't have time to do it. This kind of thinking turns our whole life into a horror. It causes high anxiety and low spirits.

We can keep thinking about these noticings and get more and more stressed. Or we can simply do these small, isolated things as we notice them, and get a shot of accomplishment each time. Instead of using the noticing about the lamp table being dusty to get us started worrying about the fact that the whole house is dirty, and we don't have time to clean the whole house, we can just get a cloth and clean the darn table. We can pay the one bill that started us worrying. We can do the one report.

See a problem, fix a problem, watch the problem go

The next thing we may notice after cleaning the table is a tub that screams: "DIRTY." We can just clean the tub. It would not be a bad housework plan to just trust that the mind will notice things as they need to be done. We can do them at the time we notice them. We don't even have to do the noticings immediately. Just make a mental note to do the small job as soon as you can fit it in. In the mere mental scheduling of something, the mind will feel that something is being done and relax.

The day before Christmas dinner, I noticed the silver forks and serving spoons were in need of polishing. My first thought was I don't have time to polish all the silver or I will be up all night. I began to stress about it. It was late, but I started in anyway, beginning with the forks and serving pieces. The rest of it didn't look all that bad. So I quit and went to bed.

A lot of work is like that. It's the tip of the iceberg that is stressing us out, but sometimes if we take care of the tip, the rest of the iceberg leaves us alone, stresswise. After I did the silver that bothered me in the first place, my mind didn't notice any other pieces of silver that needed to be polished, so I didn't end up having to clean it all. Maybe it all wasn't super-duper shiny. But my mind didn't notice, and my eyes didn't go looking for trouble. That's good enough for me.

EXERCISE #23: FOCUS ON THE ACTUAL

Don't let your thoughts go beyond your situation. A lot of stress can be avoided if we think about those things we are doing at the moment and avoid thinking about things we have done in the past or might do in the future. As much as possible we should not let our thoughts wander passively beyond our present reality. This doesn't mean you can't actively plan some course of action that is to take place in the future. Or study some course of action in the past to see where you went wrong. Studying and planning would be a legitimate present-reality situation. Too often however, we worry about past and future events when there is no productive mental or physical action we can take in present reality.

Twenty-one

Re-Engagement
Exercises

Re-engagement exercises can help change the self-focused, paranoid kind of thinking that tends to alienate us from others, and from present reality. Some of our thinking habits are not good for connecting with others.

EXERCISE #1: I AM DYING; YOU ARE DYING

I learned this exercise from Anthony de Mello. It is extremely powerful. When we self-focus, we become alienated from the people around us. This is an empty, lonely and painful feeling. We imagine all kinds of cold and unfriendly things about others, and what they might or might not be thinking about us, how we don't like or admire them.

Here is a wonderful way to reconnect with your fellow man, to put you back in touch with yourself in a more grounded way. The exercise stops you from comparing yourself, either favorably or unfavorably to others. It keeps you from being bitter about what you have or don't have. It quickly puts you on the path of charity, acceptance, community and cosmic harmony. It reminds us that although we may be different, each of us has the same inscrutable past and the same uncertain future. We are all born and we will all die.

Here's the exercise: When you meet an acquaintance that you have found hard to be with in the past for some reason, or a new person that you are unsure of, say to yourself: "I am dying and this person is dying, too." Try to experience the full meaning of the words you are saying.

EXERCISE #2: HERE COME DE JUDGE

I still have a natural, unfortunate tendency to judge people. Maybe it's part of my caveman genetics for "survival of the herd." Is this person "my kind," "my tribe," "unimportant," "alien?" I am working very hard on this because I would like to be a more loving person.

A week or so ago I was waiting in line for movie tickets with my husband and ahead of me was this very ordinary looking black man, maybe in his early 50s. I am white and a bit older. I started discounting him immediately. I realized that I didn't care a hoot about him. He was nothing to me. I wouldn't care if he disappeared off the face of the earth. And then I started to think about the World Trade Center where people who were total strangers risked their lives for each other. I wondered if something like that would make me care about this person.

My mind kind of drifted into an imaginary scenario but it wasn't a World Trade Center scene that popped up. Instead, the whole world had been destroyed and this black man and I were the last two people alive on earth. We were sitting across from each other at a small table, in a small, sparsely furnished room, dimly lit by a kerosene lamp. We were intently playing a game of Scrabble, just to pass the time of day and amuse ourselves. I looked at the man again. Funny. I cared about him now as a fellow human being. I liked him. He seemed like a nice guy. He was important to me. I felt more connected to the rest of the world as well.

Since that time I have often come across people, especially women, in whom I normally wouldn't be interested either because of their age, or the way they were dressed. I try to imagine them sitting across from me having tea in their own home, where I am a guest. From this perspective I often imagine they might have a great deal of their own brand of wisdom to share with me.

EXERCISE #3: THE COMFORT ZONE

Here's a little exercise that will help you get in touch with yourself in a very deep way. It will also help you feel more comfortable with others. We often over-ride our small feelings of discomfort or nervousness. If we do it all the time we can become disconnected from ourselves. When we become disconnected from ourselves, we also find it more difficult to connect with others. Next time you go to a meeting or party, try this: Walk around until you find "your spot" in the room. If you really pay attention to yourself you will find one place in the room where you just know you are in the right place. Try it.

I do this quite often. I might enter a room and sit down. After a couple of seconds I realize that it's not "my spot." I feel just slightly "edgy" where I am. I get up and find another seat. I am always much more comfortable and grounded.

EXERCISE #4: CONSCIOUS ARGUING:
A CLEAN GRIEF

Most of our disagreements are due to unawareness. We really don't care all that much about the outcome of our arguments. This is why we can remember so clearly how angry we were last week, last month, or even last year. And yet, we can't remember *what*, exactly, we were so angry about. We don't realize that we have a hidden agenda, a long-standing habit, to win for the sake of winning.

Here's the exercise: Plan to lose an argument the next time when you realize you are into one. Give up right away and let the other person win. It can be painful when you can't get your point accepted. Focus on the pain instead of making the point. Stay with the pain and accept it without putting the responsibility on the other person to "fix it." (That's what you want, isn't it? To get the other person to fix your pain by accepting your point?)

What you don't realize is that *seeing your pain is the real gift here.* It has been within you for a long time. No one has been hurting you. Once you become an adult, your pain is not the fault of some other person. As you accept your pain (fear is what it really is), it will finish and leave you a lighter person with much less necessity to have the last word.

This is the thing about fear. Everybody has it whether in touch with it or not. You can finish your fear if you get in touch with it and accept it. In the acceptance it dissolves. However, it will not finish if it is projected. You are projecting your pain if you think someone else is causing it. Yes, even spousal abuse. He (usually) is projecting his own pain upon you, that's all. When you handle your fear separately, you can then make a more appropriate response to the abuse. It's easier for the abusee than it is for the abuser to "get" intellectually that they are afraid. When you don't handle your fear separately, the abuse becomes a muddy projection and a distraction for both of you and neither can advance in self-awareness.

Remember, blame is the way we avoid our fear. If you want to know how afraid you are, see how often you blame your significant other for something. You don't get a pass if your blaming is all "little stuff." It will just be harder to pick it out of the atmosphere of general bickering. It is the *process*, not the *content* of the blaming that is important. When you catch yourself in some blaming, turn the focus back on yourself and look for the fear.

When you accept your fear, it becomes a clear, clean grief with no agenda, no blame, no self-pity, no engendering of sympathy except for a deep hug from the universe that you are turning to at last.

EXERCISE #5: THE EXERCISE OF LIFE

We have to relate to the world. It is not going to relate to us. The world works for us only when we make the effort to connect ourselves to it. If we withdraw from it, it becomes foreign to us. So when we feel alone and alienated, we need to activate our connection with the world no matter how hesitantly, and no matter how scary the idea is. It is often hard to bestir ourselves. It is easier to do nothing. But whether we are aware of it or not, we are the sole source of the world for ourselves, as we are the sole source of food for our bodies.

No one can eat for us, and no one can provide us with a world. Our relating to it is the switch that turns the world on for us. The world does not compel us. It might try, in the form of therapy. But the only thing a therapist uses to help us is *us*.

During one depressive episode, I spent days hiding away in the house– cemented by passivity to the unhappy walls and vacant, gloomy calm. My grandchildren came to visit and wanted to take a walk. With little enthusiasm in my heart, we started out. But after 20 minutes I woke up to the fact, with surprise, that there was a whole world I had forgotten. I'd been thinking my sad, dark house was the world. Here were the sky, the clouds, the trees. There were all these houses, and there were no doubt some nice people living in them.

Some of those people might be sad today, too, I thought, like me. I didn't know I had lost common ground with the world until I found solid earth again beneath my feet. I wished all the people well, glad that they were again part my world, and that I was part of theirs. Life does not exist intellectually, in theory; *it only exists in the actual exercise of it.*

EXERCISE #6: CONNECT WITH LIFE

Sometimes at a party or meeting, even with our own families, we suddenly feel estranged, uncomfortable, like we are not connected. We might feel that nobody cares much about us. We might feel nervous, uptight, like we don't know what to do or say next. We might feel socially inept, awkward, afraid. This is because we have allowed the focus of our attention to drift away from others and what they are saying and doing. Instead we have turned the focus to ourselves and what we are thinking and feeling.

Whenever we get too self-focused, we get self-conscious. When we are self-conscious we either get over-talkative and over-active, while inappropriately attracting attention to ourselves. Or we get quieter and quieter and withdraw into our shell. Either way is a painful position.

The first step out of this dilemma is simply to recognize it. We can say to ourselves, "I'm feeling self-conscious and disconnected so I must have become "self-absorbed." The second step is to refuse the self-focus.

You can say to yourself, "These people are not cold and unfeeling. I have lost my interest in them. These people are not distant, I have disconnected myself from them. I must refocus my attention away from my feelings and fears and start paying attention to somebody else."

We can ask someone a question and listen to their answer. Focus on them, and get our focus off us. Everybody moves along in the dark about these matters. We want to talk to people, yet we're embarrassed because we don't remember their names, so we hesitate to go up to them and start a conversation for fear we'll say the wrong thing in our ignorance of who the heck they are. The people who are better at social gatherings just have more experience at it. They have risked themselves more often and discovered that it didn't kill them when they said something stupid.

There's no magic formula. People who think there is one end up a bit phony and shallow. We just have to remember that we ourselves are persons of good will and we want to participate, and somehow we will muddle through it. We can try to recognize when we have stepped over the line, pull back, start again and be the better for the attempt. We will not always shine. Can we stand that? Usually we can redeem ourselves before we get too weird. Hey, we're all just human beings here.

EXERCISE #7: THE ESSENTIAL MESSAGE

One of my fairly new understandings is that I have to learn to make myself more accessible to the essential message that is being revealed to me when I am speaking with another person. In order to do that, I have to learn to distinguish between the essential and the non-essential.

I am beginning to see that anything I perceive as negative is non-essential to the message. Disliking something or someone, or being annoyed by something or someone, is only the product of my own attitude, my own denial, my own fear, my own precipitous judgment. It has nothing to do with their message to me.

My judgment of the message is not the same thing as the message itself. But if I'm concerned with how much I don't like something, or believe it's not worth my while, or if I am annoyed by it, then I will miss some essential message because I will have blocked it. I will have blocked my opportunity to receive the essential message by my preoccupation with the non-essential.

EXERCISE #8: WE'RE MEANER THAN WE THINK

We are getting to be an unforgiving culture because we are not very self-questioning. We can very well see that there is a bell curve for beauty by looking in the mirror. So we don't expect complete physical perfection in our nearest and dearest. They don't have to look *completely* like movie stars.

But because we can't so easily see our own *psychological imperfections,* we don't see that there is a bell curve for psychological perfection as well. Because we tend to think that we ourselves are perfectly reasonable, we expect our significant others to be perfectly reasonable as well. We do not see any reason for them to lose their tempers, to put us down, to whine and complain, or not to be ready for sex when we are.

If our significant other is being mean to us, there is a good chance it is payback for some smallness on our part that we didn't even notice because the meanness we perpetrate on our significant other is usually entirely different from the meanness they perpetrate upon us. As my sister-in-law used to put it: "Girls pinch, boys punch."

EXERCISE #9: LIVING IN THE WORLD AS WE FIND IT

We must live the life we have, not the life we would rather have. The to-be-improved life is always in the future. We can't live in the future, only today. This sounds like a pretty self-evident platitude. But if we really believed it, we would understand that we can't wait to treat our significant others lovingly until they change for the better. And it is hard, even painful at first, to be nice and pleasant to somebody when we are disappointed and angry with them. It's like betraying ourselves. And indeed it is betraying our minds.

Our minds already have decided we're going to do life the same way we have always done life. It's scary to try something new. It's scary just to be upbeat when your mind says, "Things are not right here and they need to be improved before I can relax my guard."

So the way to get started is to act like we love our nearest and dearest even when we don't. Pretend there is no other time but this NOW. So we might as well do something positive with it as if "it's all there is." It's hard, but the outcome is surprising. Usually you just have to make a small effort before things kind of progress on their own.

What is happening is that you are using your mind to engage in risking to live life, instead of letting your mind use you to disengage from life for the mind's sense of comfort. You are telling your mind you want to do something new, instead of following your mind's old habits.

Think about it. We are not rude, angry, and dismissive to the murderer who's going to be executed tomorrow. We are full of forbearance. We ask him what he wants for dinner. We fix him a nice meal, with napkins and wine. We smile, are polite, engage in light conversation. Maybe we could treat our flawed, erring, still-in-the-doghouse significant other as good as that murderer. How come we feel like it will kill us to do this? What will be killed in us? Maybe our fear will be killed.

EXERCISE #10: TELLING OTHER PEOPLE WHAT THEIR FAULTS ARE

I have been asked the question, "How do you let people know that they have these terrible faults without hurting their feelings?" My answer, "Very carefully." Since it is so hard to see our own stuff even when we are looking for it, how much harder is it to accept this kind of negative feedback from someone else? As a therapist, one of the ways I got in touch with some of my own terrible flaws was to see them evidenced over and over again in the people coming into my counseling office.

But how to show their faults to people, who have not asked you to treat them, mentor them, or criticize them, is tricky. Taking a clue from my experience as a therapist, I suggest that the best way to show person **A** some fault of his is to point out that same fault in persons **B** and **C**. Take bad table manners. You might ask **A**, "Hey, if you see me slurp my food the way that **B** and **C** are doing right now please let me know." Then if **A** slurps his food you could say, "Hey you're slurping your food just like **B**. I hate it when he does that." See, you're not saying, "I hate it when YOU do that."

But since you have asked for criticism yourself, don't be surprised when you get a dose of the same medicine and person **A** suddenly becomes free and easy with their negative comments about you.

As a general rule what works best to help improve the behavior of our nearest and dearest, both children and adults, is to reward the behavior we wish to see continued, and to ignore the behavior we wish to see extinguished. Reprehensible behavior stops when the consequences of it are raised to the point that the perpetrator prefers to drop the behavior rather than suffer the consequences.

Twenty-two

Self-Improvement Exercises

By reaching for excellence and precision in small things you improve the entire character of your larger life.

EXERCISE #1: THE INSPECTOR GENERAL

We do many things carelessly out of habit. But we can decide at any minute, as an exercise, to do them mindfully. This helps rescue some of our life from the auto-pilot state. Just simple things like straightening the book we are putting on the desk so that it is exactly even with the edge of the desk, not just any-which-way. If we are paying a bill, we can write the check neatly this time, and address the letter using our best penmanship. If we are finished with our towel we can fold it precisely before we hang it up. Any conscious act pulls us a little more from our state of unconscious oblivion to the present moment.

I often think of the late Christopher Reeve as I am midway through dashing off a hurried thank-you note to a friend, or writing out monthly bills. How would Christopher Reeve have treasured the opportunity to address a letter? After the equestrian accident which paralyzed him, wouldn't it have been the most exciting, wondrous gift to him to be able to lift his arm and move his hand deliberately across the paper? Wouldn't it have seemed the greatest miracle to write down an address? And here I am rushing through it as if it doesn't matter a whit. Then I will start to notice, myself, the great privilege it is to be able to hold a pen in my hand and write. It is a miracle. I do my very best.

Philosophers of old were on the right track in their simple and straightforward trust that the work of our hand should always be the best we can do. Modern neuroscience clearly shows that deliberate activity "works" to eliminate falling into subcortical depression by stimulating neural activity in the neocortex.

The 19th-century Catholic priest R. W. Faber anticipated neuroscience when he taught, "Exactness in little things is a wonderful source of cheerfulness." He understood the principle long before anybody understood the science behind it. Concentrating upon being exact is neocortical activity, and feelings of gloom do not reside in the neocortex. Only the subcortex has the capacity for despair. Small duties, thoughtfully performed, can move us out of self-focus into a larger community with the cosmos where we feel more connected with present reality.

EXERCISE #2: MAKE-OVER

Add one item to personal grooming that would ordinarily not be done just for "work" or "around the house." It doesn't matter how small a change. Again, the goal is strengthening the process of doing something we don't want to do in order to exercise our will over the status-quo mind that tells us we don't care.

It's not *we* who don't care. It's our guardian, safety-conscious, habitual mind that doesn't care. It wants us to hide our light under a bushel so nobody will take a pot shot at us when we try to stand up and "take our space." The habitual mind fears courage. The habitual mind is happy and secure when it can anticipate "what's next." Since there is no way to anticipate the outcome of a courageous act, the mind tries to rein us in when we come to those forks in the road where we have an opportunity to take the "high road." That's why we're often afraid to "do the right thing."

EXERCISE #3: DIRTY LAUNDRY LIST

Keep a list of all the rationalizations that the instinctive defensive mind will stack up for you in order to further excuse you from doing things you don't feel like doing. (I'll do it later, I'm owed two minutes because I did a four-minute chore yesterday, etc.) Notice how clever the rationalizations can get. Talk about outsmarting ourselves! Our defensive mind is in an end run around us to seduce us into running our lives by habit, rather than by decision; by feeling, instead of principle. If it cannot avoid innovative activity entirely, it will create persuasive rationalizations for postponing non-habitual actions. "Not today, I'm feeling a little tired. I'll do it tomorrow."

Don't be surprised if your defensive mind comes up with a clever rationalization for not doing the make-over exercise just above. "Maybe it's not such a good idea to place undue importance on *outer beauty*." Sound familiar? That's not your internal value system at work; it's your instinctive defensive mind trying to keep you safely within the boundaries of habit.

EXERCISE #4: JUST DO IT

At the same time every day, do one small chore that you don't want to do, a chore that will bring a little order to your surroundings. This chore should take two minutes or less. It does not need to be a complete chore. For instance, you may not be able to organize all your files, but you could put all the bills in one folder, and file the folder. If this exercise represents something entirely new for you, you will be very resistant to it. You will rationalize not doing it by saying that it is stupid, and it won't do any good, and won't make any difference. Do it anyway. The idea here is process rather than content. It doesn't matter *what* you do; it just matters *that you do it*. The idea is to start over-riding habitual mindsets by an act of will.

EXERCISE #5: MANIA, MANIA. WHEREFORE ART THOU, MANIA?

When the next "Great Idea" shows up, check out the level of accompanying excitement. Excitement has nothing to do with whether the idea is any good or not, only whether or not we are more or less likely to carry it out. It is easy to confuse excitement with "worth." Think of at least three other "Great Ideas" that generated great initial excitement that didn't live up to our expectations. How is the current idea so different from those? Is there any doubt and insecurity? Doubt and insecurity always accompany rational thinking. Think again! Mania cannot withstand self-questioning. Self-questioning is the sober antidote to mania. But trying to get other people to see their own mania is almost impossible. For the person who will not question themselves, nothing can be done.

EXERCISE #6: STICKS AND STONES CAN BREAK MY BONES BUT WORDS WILL NEVER HURT ME!

Notice how we feel "hurt" when someone criticizes us or points their anger or aggression in our direction. Write down the reasons we feel emotionally "hurt" and see how rational they *aren't*. It is *normal* to feel hurt, even though it is irrational. So let our understanding of hurt give us a bit of balance in undergoing it. Hurt is not a great big deal. It is just a normal, everyday kind of thing that we endure as part of the human condition. We all have terrible flaws. So we "hurt" each other now and then.

Anger is fear turned outward. Emotional hurt is fear turned inward. If we know this, then we can be more self-questioning about our hurt. Once we have the intellectual understanding that hurt is fear, hurt will begin disappearing as one of our life's experiences. People's outrageous behavior will not be experienced by us as "hurting our feelings," it will be seen as their outrageous behavior.

Until we understand that "hurt" is really our own fear turned back upon ourselves, our lives will constantly be at the mercy of mean, selfish, thoughtless, inconsiderate or abusive people. We will exhaust ourselves trying to justify our beliefs and actions to these people, trying to fix these people, trying to change them, and trying to placate them so that they will stop doing or saying the things that hurt us. Instead, we should concentrate on taking care of ourselves in a reasonable, appropriate way when difficult situations arise.

Once our eyes are open to the psychological realities of "hurt," we will realize that the rude and inconsiderate people to whom, in our fear, we have given so much power are really just socially inept. They are unknowing rather than mean, immature rather than inconsiderate. Of course, there are people in the world who are just plain selfish and they really don't care much about us. But we are foolish to waste our time translating their personal shortcomings into our own pain.

All chronic abusive situations are caused by fear. The abuser turns his or her fear outward, and aggresses. The victim accepts the aggression and turns it inward as emotional hurt. Except for physical battery (here, one should call 911), abusive people cannot psychologically or emotionally inflict "hurt" upon you. You have to do that yourself by turning their aggression (their fear turned outward) inward upon yourself. You do this out of your lack of courage to take care of yourself in adverse situations. This is another example of blame being the way we avoid seeing our own fear.

EXERCISE #7: WELL, EXCUUUUZE ME!

Experiencing the ignominy and pain of a faux pas, or a social mistake is a wonderful way to learn to not take ourselves so seriously. The experience of embarrassment willingly undergone is a true pilgrim's progress of the soul. To just stand there quietly and let ourselves reverberate with the electric shock of it. It feels like we are dying. But it isn't us that's dying. It is only our fear dying. You think our fear, our most intimate companion, is going to leave us like a thief in the night? Nope. It will give us a bear hug first. We handle fear by greeting it like an old friend, and letting it wash through us like a wave. If we want we can float on the wave. This is especially good for the problem of agoraphobia. We can just float right out the door.

EXERCISE #8: WANNABE LIST

For five minutes write down a list of what you want out of life that you don't have. Then write down on the opposite side of your conscious wants each thing that you are now doing that you *don't want*. They are your wants also even though you may claim that you did not choose them. They only exist because your other list is not actively being pursued.

EXERCISE #9: TRACKING BEHAVIOR

Think about what standards we should test our ideas against. For instance: is what we are about to do going to further our life goals? Or is it merely tangential to them? Or worse, is it a step in the opposite direction of our goals? Are we doing something just to make us feel good, or are we intending to do some good? Remember that *feeling good* is much more exciting than *doing good*. If it's really for charity then it won't be all that exciting.

EXERCISE #10: TRACKING BEHAVIOR #2

It is often an eye-opener to write a list of the five things we value most. Then write down next to them how many minutes of a normal day are devoted to our most important values. Then we can write down a list of things we do that we don't think highly of. Write down next to them how many minutes of a normal day are devoted to these things we don't much care about.

EXERCISE #11: THE UNIVERSAL LAW

This exercise did not originate with me by any means. I learned it when I took a course in Silva Mind Control, so I will credit it to them although I believe it is probably much older than any 20th-century wisdom. You get back from the universe only what you have first given it freely. So if you want love, you must first give love. If you want money, you must first give money. What do you want from life? Whatever you want, first give it!

This exercise is reminiscent of the real circumstance of having to pour some water into the pump first in order to prime it before you start to draw water from the well. There's a wonderful old country song about this. A thirsty man comes across a well in the desert with a full bottle of water next to it. On the bottle is a note to warn the traveler not to drink the water in the bottle to slack his thirst, but to use the water to prime the pump.

> *You've got to prime the pump. You must have faith and*
> *believe.*
> *You've got to give of yourself 'fore you're worthy to receive.*
> *Drink all the water you can hold. Wash your face, cool your*
> *feet.*
> *But leave the bottle full for others. Thank you kindly, Desert Pete.*

EXERCISE #12: THE DEVIL IS IN THE DECISION

We don't always realize, when we do things that are not in our best interest, that we do them because we have simply not made any specific, current, here-and-now decision about them. If we are not in a decision mode concerning some next action, we will just go with what has become habit. Too often that means bad habit. For instance, I noticed that after the holidays this year I had to lie down on my bed to zip up my jeans. I decided I needed to lose some weight. After a couple of days I realized that I hadn't lost any weight.

One night I asked myself (after I ate them), "Why am I still eating chocolates?"

"Well," I responded to myself, "did I make a decision, tonight, not to eat any?" Of course I had not made that decision. I realized that although I had made a general, indefinite-as-to-hour-or-minute decision to not eat chocolates, when the time came and dinner was over I just walked to the kitchen and ate them out of habit. (Well I also ate them out of greed and gluttony, but these are bad habits also, right?) Bad habits can always be derailed by good decisions.

Here's the exercise: The next night I asked myself as I was eating dinner, "Now, have I made a decision not to eat chocolates this evening?" I realized that I hadn't yet made a definite decision about this very current situation. So I made one. I decided to abstain from the chocolates. (The mind can't do a no, so it is very important to make decisions based on some kind of a yes or we won't have the same control over our mind.) The mind will try to do what we are asking, but it has to turn any no into a yes before it can do it. So it is for that reason, at the moment of decision, I said "to abstain" rather than "just say no." I know this is a fine straw but so are our neurons.

For support in my decision, I leaned on one of Shakespeare's lines: which I appropriated for the occasion, "Abstain tonight and that will make tomorrow's abstinence that "much easier." (The actual line is "Refrain tonight and that shall lend a kind of easiness to the next abstinence.") It worked. I didn't eat the chocolates that night. I immediately decided to perfect my decision-making, now that I was onto something helpful.

Remember to ask yourself if you made a decision

The next day, on the way to lunch with friends I asked myself, "Have I now decided to have the fruit plate for lunch instead of the tempting, open-faced turkey sandwich with gravy, mashed potatoes and cranberry sauce that this little café is famous for?" (For the last two lunches I have had the turkey despite my general intention, in advance, to have something less fattening.) It is better to give the mind a "Get the fruit" rather than a "No turkey." I ordered the fruit successfully this time.

I lost 3 pounds in a week and a half. Not much maybe, but I might have gained 3 pounds instead. Then I would have eleven pounds to lose. As it was I had only five more pounds to go. Now we shouldn't horrible-ize it if we have a lot more pounds to lose. Pounds are lost one at a time, not twenty or fifty at a time. If we keep taking care of the tip of the iceberg, pretty soon the entire iceberg will disappear.

As often as I remember it, and I am trying to program this into long-term memory, when I reach for the chocolates or the pie, I ask myself, "Have I actually made a decision to eat this?" I think I almost embarrass myself. I almost always abstain when I question myself. And it is getting harder and harder for my appetite thoughts to sneak past the questioning thoughts without getting caught.

Give the mind a task and it will complete it

My thoughts of dessert, and my automatic reach for them have started to form a strong neuronal connection with the thought "Have I made a decision about this?" The question spotlights the struggle between my appetite and my willpower (the choice of long-term gains over short term gains). Gluttony doesn't get so much of a free ride anymore. And some of my decisions are turning into good habits. All habits, good or bad, begin as a single decision. As a further support for this exercise I often think "Every day, in every way, I am eating healthier and healthier."

One interesting thing about making a decision is that the mind is such a dutiful servant that, once we have made a decision and insist upon it, the mind will, on its own, do all in its power to carry it out. It is perfectly all right to make a decision to do something, even if we don't have the slightest idea how we are going to actually do it, and leave the details up to the mind. This little fact is already working against us when we *don't* make a decision. When we let the mind make our decisions for us, it has the full disposal, through learned association, of the totality of our experience, knowledge, talents, weaknesses, and can use all of these things to keep us stuck in a bad habit.

When we make a decision to do something new, and insist upon it, repetitiously, over and over, the mind, being a problem solver, will avail itself of everything it possesses to solve the problem of how to carry out our decision. I've occasionally used this make-a-decision idea to get to sleep by telling my mind "I'm asleep now" and relaxing, letting the mind figure out how to get me to where I have decided I am.

We must get nosy about what we are doing

One of the reasons we don't effect good changes in our lives is because we seem to be in some kind of a self-conspiracy not to know what the heck we are doing. It takes a purposeful, conscious effort to see what we are up to; to notice what we are thinking. One of the best ways I know to find out what we are up to is to ask ourselves, "Have I made a decision about this?" It takes us off automatic pilot and puts us squarely in front of ourselves.

Being on automatic pilot all the time enables us to have violent tempers and yet think of ourselves as pussy cats. It causes us to gain weight before we know what has happened. It allows us to drift into depression because we don't notice those first negative, downer thoughts when we could more easily drop them, before they have a good power-hold over us.

Not knowing what we are doing is an automatic self-defense strategy of our mind to maintain the status quo, no matter how terrible it is and no matter how much we hate it. The mind trusts the status quo because we have so far "survived" in it. And the status quo reigns supreme until we make a decision to change it. This is why we usually opt for the "known," and greatly fear the possibly-better unknown. Thus the mind has us thinking in circles instead of focusing exactly on what we are doing. *We don't want to know the simple problems of our lives* because the defensive mind doesn't want us to solve the simple problem and thus change the status quo.

Addiction to anything, whether food, depression, alcohol, gambling or sex, sets in because we turn down our wick of awareness on certain behaviors—so that we can more easily continue them, and maintain what has accidentally become the defensive mind's status quo. As psychologist Nathaniel Branden says, "self-destruction is an act best performed in the dark."

Our defensive mind wants us to chain ourselves with voluntary ignorance to "keep us safe." *The defensive mind is secure in our habitual behavior and our addictions.* Of course this does not make any rational sense. We have to remember that intelligence is not one of the strategies of the defensive mind. Its great strategy is fear. Intelligence is a strategy of our reason.

The defensive, guardian mind likes the status quo, such as addictions

That old reptilian brain, the first mind system to evolve, mistakenly believes that as original "Godfather," he should be in charge of us. It is absolutely dedicated, and is not going to give way without cunning on our part to limit the over-extension of his only strategies: feelings and fear. When we find ourselves going habitual we can ask ourselves, "Wait a minute, have I truly made a decision about this?"

Decisions to avoid temptation are more efficient the further distance from temptation that they can be made. For instance, I have always said that the difference between me and a 300 pound woman is only at the grocery store. If I buy a pie and bring it home, I am not going to throw it away. Eventually I will eat it. Now, by decision, I can eat it over a period of two weeks which will mitigate the damage to my health, but eat it, sooner or later, I will.

Similarly, if one is prone to gambling in excess, the decision to avoid the casino is better than the decision, once in the casino, not to gamble more than twenty dollars. And we can strengthen our decision-making process with little mind tricks as well. I always eat just before I go grocery shopping so that I'm not hungry. Hunger is very tempting when eyeing a chocolate layer cake.

EXERCISE #13: THE POOL OR PILLOW SCREAM

This exercise provides some emotional release for us fraidy cats and shrinking violets who've been repressing our feelings for years because we don't want to make anybody mad at us. It seldom occurs to us that we are playing the game of life with different rules from those other people who don't care if they hurt *our* feelings or make *us* mad at *them*. Why do we let people yell at us and lose their tempers and then not take up for ourselves?

If we are in jail it is probably a good thing to not mouth off to the guard. If we live in a totalitarian society, perhaps we have no real power. But in a free land, we have the opportunity to exercise our full freedom as a human being. We just may need to learn how to do it appropriately. We can only do things appropriately when we are not doing them out of fear. Anything we do out of fear is always, in some way, inappropriate. So the first thing to do is to become familiar with our repressed fear. That will help us become familiar with our fear on a more current, daily basis.

Here's the exercise: We can scream into a pillow, roll around on the floor. We don't have to worry about what to scream about. Once we start into the physical activity of screaming about nothing in particular, images, ideas, and old memories will start to bubble up and urge us on. It is simple, but not easy to do, for some of us who are shy about our feelings,

It took me months of working with a psychotherapist before I was able to express anger overtly as I had spent 30 years learning how to hold it back. Emotional release is not to be trotted out and thrust upon the general public in the form of road rage, or rudeness to store clerks and waiters. Nor is it to be forced upon our nearest and dearest just because we feel better after we rage at them. *They* won't feel better. We can join an emotional release group or work on it privately by ourselves.

If we find it hard to get started maybe screaming into a pillow is too much. We could try low groaning or moaning, a sad kind of weaving side-to-side dance. Work up to the screaming part. We can do this in private; nobody has to see us. But this work will have to be done sooner or later if we are to live our lives fully, and not go through life constricted by our own body fear.

I have also done emotional release sessions with a group of people who were all working together on expressing long held-in feelings and emotion. To drum beats we moaned and groaned and rolled around on the floor. We spread out in a big auditorium and wore masks over our eyes so we didn't see each other and intrude on one another. The energy of the group made a more powerful experience than any of us would have had working alone. But alone is better than not doing it at all.

Emotional release gives us objectivity about feelings

If we have access to a swimming pool, we can get under water and scream our anguish, depression, disappointment and guilt until we can get it all out of our system. It's very freeing.

This is a good exercise to see how, by an act of will, we can move a lot of feelings right out of our body that have been hanging around fermenting and making us stale. Avoiding our emotional pain can ultimately make us sick. But feeling pain per se can't hurt us when we accept it while we're feeling it.

It's the avoiding the feeling of pain that kills us because those feelings we have repressed are in our very muscles and sinews. This repression has to be felt and released with a little playacting so we can quit carrying it around. It's unnecessary and dangerous baggage.

The pool and pillow scream are especially wonderful when we feel like jumping out of our skin with tension, anger, frustration, or anguish. It provides immediate physical relief from anxiety and stress. Sometimes we make horrible mistakes. We get fired; we make stupid remarks and feel guilty. Sometimes terrible things happen to us or to our loved ones. Thinking about these terrible things cause painful, terrifying feelings to rise up in our bodies, and we grab for something to anesthetize ourselves so we don't hurt.

We're not hurting, our *feelings* are hurting. We need to learn how to distance ourselves from our feelings so we can be more objective about their reality. So we can distinguish ourselves from our feelings instead of thinking we are our feelings or that our feelings are us. By doing these exercises we can begin to feel like the owner and guardian of our feelings instead of their victim.

EXERCISE #14: LAUGH AND THE WORLD LAUGHS WITH YOU

To get some distance between us and our feelings laugh silently for 10 minutes, out loud if you're alone. This will be hard because we think such things are stupid and hokey, and we won't want to do it for more than about 3 seconds. "Oh, it's not working," we'll say right away. But keep doing it; it is especially powerful to laugh out loud. Any kind of laugh. Notice the kinds of laughs that will come up: a shy laugh, a this-is-stupid-laugh, a big fake belly laugh, an obedient laugh, an I-hate-to-laugh laugh, a high laugh, a sing-song laugh, a low laugh. This seldom works on the first attempt. Don't give up on the exercise. Do it again another time.

When we finally insist on doing this exercise all the way we start to feel just a little light-hearted, no matter how low or stale or angry or resistant we feel when we start. Also, from the repetition of all those phony laughs, we usually accomplish at least one legitimate laugh and that surprises the heck out of us, and at the same time we see that some small mood change has occurred.

The point of this exercise is not to make us happy. The point of this exercise is to see how we can direct small changes in our feelings, which are not all that laughable when we begin, and that we can do it on purpose, regardless of what our mind wants us to do. Our mind will not want us to laugh. Our mind will object strenuously to this exercise. If we do it anyway, we'll learn a lot.

EXERCISE #15: OKAY. I GIVE UP.

Another name for this exercise is Surrender to Reality. When I wrote something about it on a slip of paper and stuck it in a drawer somewhere like I always do, and later found it, it said: "I dare to ride out into the vast desert of my lonely self, sit down, and wait for death."

Someone asked me once if I kept a writer's journal. I said no, that I kept "writer's scraps." Another slip of paper that turned up on the same subject said: "If your world is truly empty, you will not be able to hide so easily from your own soul." Here's one more scrap: "How odd that the fear of a thing hurts, but the reality of it never does." *That has been my experience: reality never hurts.*

So if you are hurting, you are not in present reality, you have slipped into some emotional turmoil of the subcortex, and are caught up some kind of instant replay of old stuff.

Which has lead me to the conclusion that feelings should never be confused with objective reality.

Here's the exercise: I remember once feeling terribly betrayed by a good friend. I got so depressed I thought I was going to die. In the past, things like this had bothered and depressed me for two or three years at a time. I just decided that since the pain would end finally in three years anyway, why couldn't I just do it all at once, and end it in three weeks instead, so I wouldn't "waste another three years of my life?"

So, resolutely, I lay down on my bed and invited "The Beast of Pain." "Okay. Give me all you've got, right now. If it kills me, I'll just die. Whatever you're going to throw at me for the next three years to make my life miserable, give it to me *NOW*. I'm ready to suffer." I concentrated as hard as I could on feeling it all. I didn't want any pain to escape and come back to haunt me later. After about twenty minutes, all the depression was pretty much gone.

For some reason I had decided that I could compress the entire experience, and just be in pain for three weeks. I don't know why I selected that particular interval of time. But it worked. In the next two weeks I would get waves of it, but I went through the same surrender scene and, although quite ready to endure much longer, it usually only lasted about twenty minutes. Sometimes it lasted only two or three minutes. I was surprised. After three weeks, I was over the whole thing. I would feel around and see if I could come up with any twinges of pain or regret, but it was finished.

EXERCISE #16: ONCE MORE, WITH FEELING

This exercise is to show us that feelings, our defense mechanisms, are susceptible to change as our body moves around. Feelings are biochemical reactions that happen to our body. Sometimes we think our feelings are paralyzing us. Believe it or not, that's exactly what they are doing.

Wilhelm Reich was the first to call attention to our "skeletal body armor" caused by the contracted muscles and restricted breathing resulting from the habitual postures we take. The postures are our response to fearful feelings that aren't allowed to finish themselves in some kind of forward action that restores our sense of okayness.

The psychological responses of repressed feelings can thus become somaticized in the body. That is, physical postures that we take by shrugging or cringing, and mental postures that we take in avoiding or blaming can, over time, be reflected in changes to ourselves on a cellular level.

Painful memories are thus stored in the tissues of our body. It is so heartbreaking to see small children or teenagers with their shoulders all bent in and their chest caved hollow, in that protective posture that bespeaks a hurt heart.

Unfinished feelings may be released during simple playacting which mimics the completion of forward action that was stopped originally.

Here's the exercise: When we shake them up, the residue of unexpressed feelings can come loose, move through our body, and finish themselves. Dancing them out is good. Running them out is good. One of my favorite exercises, when I start obsessing about some stupid thing I have done, or some indignity I have experienced, is to get down on my hands and knees and groan out loud. I mean, really groan and thrash around like an animal. I can howl like a wolf. I can get angry and grizzly without any need to be angry and grizzly *at anything, or anyone in particular.* Of course it is always some specific person or incident that gets me going, but soon the situation becomes generalized. Thus some current incident can put me in touch, body wise, with ancient emotional history.

This exercise puts us in touch with our emotions in a way which counteracts our automatic connection with them. Too often we are simply automatons, erupting in feelings that we don't even know we are having even while we are having them. We don't even know that we are angry or scared. We don't know we are taking postures which are threatening or cringing. We are just reacting in some automatic, habitual way.

I like to do this in private. It doesn't seem the kind of thing to do in front of an audience. (Although I have been in groups where everyone is blindfolded and dancing and groaning out their pain, and it is very powerful.) Your mind, your chief operating defense mechanism, will not want you to mess with your repressed feelings by groaning, groveling, and growling on your hands and knees like a wild animal. Do it anyway.

EXERCISE #17: DO NOT THINK OF AN ELEPHANT.

Do not think of an elephant. This is an old proverb, that there is no way *not* to think of an elephant. The way we do not think about an elephant is to choose something *else* to think about and think about that. Choose some other thought *other than* elephant. The mind can only entertain one thought at a time, and we can choose that thought. It does take some wrestling with our mind to achieve sovereignty over which thought will prevail. Our thought or "elephant." Our thought or our mind's. This is an exercise in concentration upon a single thought. Our thought.

EXERCISE #18: THE ROAD WE DO TAKE

If you live on a small side street that you travel from your home to the highway, watch your speedometer, and limit your speed to no more than 15 miles per hour on this road. At first you will be annoyed and racing ahead in your mind. As you continue to do the exercise you will see how your whole system slows down, becomes less anxious; your back relaxes and comes back down; you enjoy the small scenes, a neighbor's cut grass, a tree, the skyline. Another byproduct is that you will be leaving more on time since you know you can't make up for it on this road. This road is sacred. Perhaps this idea will expand until we can see that this whole existence is sacred.

EXERCISE #19: CHANGE YOUR ENTIRE LIFE IN ONE HOUR

Now maybe this is not an exercise we want to do all the time. But to do this even once can put us in touch with something essential about human existence that usually eludes us. There is something truly magical about our life that we don't catch because we are caught up in judging our life. Judging life is not the same thing as living life and this exercise gives some essential clue that life may be more than it seems, and time may be less than it seems.

This is a great exercise for the middle of the day when we are unhappy that we have not accomplished what we wanted to with the morning and we feel dissatisfied with the day in particular, ourselves and life in general, and worried about time wasted again, opportunities passing us by, and we feel very behind the clock. We're disappointed in ourselves. We feel lazy and incompetent. Therefore we don't even enjoy the free time we have "right now" because it is all clogged up with guilt for how we could be enjoying it now if we'd just "done more earlier."

We can continue with the rest of the day and feel vaguely unfinished and unsettled or we can decide to change everything and have our life just the way we want in one hour. How? For example, say it is 2PM on Sunday afternoon and we meant to exercise, but we didn't. We didn't bother to dress very well either, we were planning to do that *after* we exercised. So we feel basically scrubby and unhappy with the day and with ourselves. We probably wish that we had done our exercises and gotten dressed, right?

Suppose you could have your wish, but it would happen an hour later. Would that still be good? Of course! Did you ever think that we can wave a magic wand like our own fairy godmother and have exactly what we want in just one hour?

Your whole life changes as soon as you realize that *you* are the one you have been waiting for.

Here's the exercise: Look at your watch and wish you had exercised. Now, make the wish come true. Exercise *now*.

We can do something instead of worrying that we didn't do it. Did you know that? What good is knowing something if we don't put it into action? We can forget about the first part of the day. Chuck the whole thing; it wasn't all that great anyway. Besides, it's already gone, whether we chuck it or not. And we can have a great "rest of the day" in just one hour. We can take every bit of energy we're expending to beat ourselves up for not exercising before, and put it to use exercising right now. This is really magic. Magic! But like all magic, we have to work to turn the trick.

You may think this is silly. But what's really silly is feeling bad for the rest of the day about not having accomplished something in the first hour of the day. Silly, because we could do right now in an hour what will change the whole day. Believe me, if you do the exercise, you won't think it is silly.

EXERCISE #20: AS THE TWIG IS BENT

This is an exercise that my son and daughter-in-law use in their holistic health schools, Healing Hands. It demonstrates graphically the effect that our physical body has on our mind. Once we're aware of the intimate connection between our physical body and our emotions, we can manipulate the body to effect a change upon our emotions. This exercise will teach us the body-mind connection by "playing" with it.

Here's the exercise: Assume different postures and hold them while you become aware of feelings that arise that are congruent with the postures. Hunch over like a frightened victim and hold the position. Soon victim-like feelings will arise. Stand with both feet apart and lift clenched hands up like a fighter stance, with a belligerent scowl and feelings of power or anger will surface. Hug yourself and sway gently in a soothing way. Compassion will arise. Weep and wail silently, and thrash around until despair arises. Mourn silently until sadness appears. Shield yourself, scream silently and protest as if being attacked. Fear will arise. The lesson from these postures is how subservient feelings are. How quickly they can change when you provide a different situation, idea or context for the body.

EXERCISE #21: TAKING JOY

Like most people perhaps, I had long thought that joy was rare and came on its own, at magical moments, like when you won the lottery or fell in love. I thought of Joy as something you got, not something you *did*. Then I listened to a talk which ended with the speaker saying, "Why can't we just take joy in that fact?"

Until then I never thought about joy as something one *took*, like taking a bath or taking a walk. Could it be as true for joy as it is true for courage and liberty, and conscience? These things, too, *only* come in the *exercise* of them. You don't *get* them from somewhere, you *do* them.

Being grateful for liberty is not the same thing as the lump in our throat when we hear the Star-Spangled Banner. Knowing the difference between right and wrong is not the same thing as returning the money when the cashier gives us too much change. An intellectual understanding of courage is not the same thing as facing someone's righteous anger with nothing but the small pitiful truth in our hand.

Could joy be an exercise?

I know we can decide to stop lying. I know that we can change the way we do things in order to make ourselves a better person. Could we also learn to exercise joy so we could have it on purpose? I felt like an entomologist in the wilderness with my net poised over a rare and elusive butterfly. For starters, who better to study than myself?

Early Sunday morning my husband asked me to get something from the patio. I stopped myself midway in my task and asked myself why wasn't I, right this second, (if we are going to study ourselves, it's best to go second-by-second) taking joy in this beautiful yard, with all the flowers blooming, a pleasant breeze, and the blue sky twinkling overhead?

My answer to myself was a surprise. I couldn't take joy because I was still in my nightgown, I hadn't dressed or fed the dogs yet, or the cats. I couldn't take joy until those things were finished, right? But am I ever "all finished? Am I ever all ready?

The next day I asked my daughter, a new mother, what she thought about taking joy in something. She said, oddly enough, that when I said the word joy, her first thought was a stab of fear. Something to do with guilt. Something to do with life *not* being joyful the way it should be.

The positive is always a risk

I think my daughter hit upon something important. We are never more naked than in a moment of joy. We are vulnerable. We can be hurt. Only the negative, the painful, is safe and comfortable, no matter how much we hate it. The positive is always a scary risk, no matter how much we long to have it.

Of course this makes sense since the mind is, evolutionarily speaking, a defense mechanism. We are therefore at home with problems, failures, with worry about things not done. Joy, being the most positive thing there is, is probably a total mystery to the mind. What good is joy to a defense mechanism? It doesn't feed us, clothe us, or shelter us from attack. It doesn't compute.

We take offence; we take aim; we take defeat; we take care; we take medicine; we take sick; but I never heard of anybody taking joy. I would have to think more about this.

A few days later, I cut some roses and brought them into the house. I like to see flowers in my house. But liking to see flowers in the house, I suddenly realized, is not real joy, is it? Even being grateful for seeing flowers all around is not the same as joy. Why don't I take joy in these flowers? I decided, then and there, with rose basket in hand, to do it.

Could I take joy on purpose?

I didn't know if I could take joy on purpose, not knowing at all how. I became quite still and silent, stopping everything, putting my whole self on pause. I took a deep breath and felt my shoulders relax with the out-breath. I surrendered my whole being to the flowers. Just went belly up.

It was as though time stopped. I felt something definitely more essential about the flowers than just liking them. It was more like love, even though it wasn't exactly head-over-heels exciting love. It was a more gentle flood of love, filling up in the area of my chest. Like a sunrise of the heart. As this was my first attempt at taking joy, I was surprised that it worked at all. It only took a second. There it was. Joy.

Shortly after this first success with taking joy, I had kind of a blah day. I had gotten some disappointing news about my vacation plans. A lunch date with a friend fell through. I was definitely not happy. Then I had this thought. I wonder if I could take joy even when I was feeling down in the dumps. I looked around to see what I could focus on, for something to take joy in. My eyes lighted on a favorite framed photo of my daughter. I decided to take joy in that picture. Darned if it didn't work. Just like the roses.

I have been taking joy, now and then, ever since that first time. It always works whenever I remember and take the time to do it. Here is my conclusion about joy. Joy is inherently available to us, on demand. Whenever we want it. Even when we're depressed. We just have to slow down. Come to a pause. Relax totally. Then look around for something to take joy in. Joy comes with the world. It's all around us. All the time. Ours to take.

EXERCISE #22: I THINK, THEREFORE I AM

Start checking up on your thinking at odd moments. Pay attention to what kind of thinking you are presently engaged in. Are you thinking objectively or subjectively? Are you thinking on-purpose or passively? Are you thinking reactively or proactively?

EXERCISE #23: MAKE IT IMPORTANT TO YOU

It is human nature that we take care of things that are important to us. So it follows, by simple logic, that if we want to accomplish anything, to drop some small habit, or acquire some small habit, that we have to make it important to us first. Otherwise we just never get around to it.

We are just fooling ourselves if we think we can remember to put our car keys on the wall hook as soon as we come in the door, or to charge our cell phones every night, unless we first decide that IT IS IMPORTANT. Your mind knows what is important to you and it "doesn't bother much" about those things you've mentally tagged as unimportant. You can fool your mind into "bothering" about small habits by making the decision that they are IMPORTANT.

EXERCISE #24: TRY NOT TO BE TOO AUTHENTIC

I met a ninety-three-year-old man at a party once. I asked him how come he looked so handsome and energetic at his age, and he responded, "Oh, I try not to be too authentic." I try to remember this as often as I can when I am out there trying to prove my worth to the world.

EXERCISE #25: THE MYTH OF EASY

It's helpful to remember that it's *easier* to stay depressed with your attention focused in the subcortex. It's *harder* to direct your thinking to the neocortex. Perhaps it seems like an insignificant point, but I have generally found that when I acknowledge that something is "not easy" I get about it with a better attitude. Admitting that something is difficult seems to call up the motivation to do it.

The reason many things are thought easy is that you generally end up *not* doing them. Things like singing a dumb nursery rhyme over and over to thought-jam the painful thought "I am depressed," seems easy. There are a lot of things that seem so easy that we dismiss them as trivial and don't do them. *Not doing them* is what is easy about them.

For example, when I decided to lose weight, I wanted to drink 8 glasses of water a day. At first, when it was time for another glass and I was busy with something, I would it put off with the thought that it was an "easy enough thing to do," I would "catch it later."

After a few days, I realized that "later" turned out to be "never." I had only drunk 2 or 3 glasses of water. I decided that it is *hard* to drink 8 glasses of water a day. When it was about time for my next glass and I was busy doing something else, I would think, "It's *hard* to drink 8 glasses of water a day, so you better do it RIGHT NOW!"

Here's the exercise: Whatever simple thing you want to accomplish that seems to elude you, say to yourself: "This is not as easy as one might think. This is hard to do, so let me decide exactly how I am going to tackle it."

EXERCISE #26: HOW TO STOP EXAGGERATING OR FIBBING

Lifetime habits form our persona. If you have decided that you exaggerate too much and that you tell fibs, just out of habit, when you could just as easily tell the truth, this exercise is for you. When you catch yourself after just telling someone something that is not quite the truth, say, right out loud, like a public announcement, "That's a lie." And then proceed to tell the truth. Or you can soften it by saying, "Oops, that's a lie."

This is the exercise I used to stop my long-standing habit of telling less than the truth. I was quite surprised that when I said, "Wait a minute, that's a lie," hardly anybody seemed to notice in the least.

Twenty-three

Exercises for Insomnia

Most people don't realize that the trouble with sleeping is that instead of thinking about going to sleep they think about NOT going to sleep. The fear about not going to sleep triggers your fight-or-flight response and the stress chemicals prevent you from relaxing. You must get out of the subcortex into the neocortex. Then from the neocortex you can fool your mind into becoming calm.

EXERCISE #1: MAKE THE PROBLEM THE SOLUTION

Suppose you are trying to get to sleep and a faucet is dripping, or there is noise outside, or somebody's snoring. Make the annoying noise into a meditation or mantra to help you get to sleep. Simply close your eyes and relax your body. Then say to yourself, "With every sound of the dripping faucet I am going deeper and deeper asleep." Hear the sound, and repeat the meditation. Visualize yourself feeling the sensation of falling every time you hear the sound. "Falling deeper and deeper. Deeper and deeper." If you use this meditation often enough you will form a neuronal pattern which will link the words "deeper and deeper" into the process of falling asleep.

EXERCISE #2: I AM ASLEEP

All of us struggle at times with insomnia, especially as we age. Human nature is such that we don't have to have big problems, or indeed any problems at all to suffer with insomnia. Sometimes a stray line of maverick thinking can spark up, magnify and entrench itself before we realize it, and cause us to toss and turn.

One evening I went out to dinner (after going out to both breakfast and lunch that day). I knew that I had no business eating that much entertainment food and I had blown my good intentions to lose some weight. No wonder when I went to bed I felt guilty. Guilt feelings are not conducive to drifting off into a peaceful sleep. Then I started worrying that, because I was worrying so much, I wouldn't be able to get to sleep and I had an early appointment in the morning. It was another breakfast. Oh, my God, I thought, I'm doomed. I decided I'd have to take charge of my mind; that I wasn't in the proper frame of mind to go to sleep.

I starting using the Just Say Yes exercise to drown out and get rid of the guilty thoughts. "Yes, yes, yes, yes, yes." That helped. I stopped actively beating myself up mentally. Then, after a minute or two, I used the Every Day, in Every Way exercise: "Every day in every way I'm getting thinner and thinner. Every Day in every way I'm getting thinner and thinner." That helped to get me to a little more positive mind place. Then I started counting backwards from 999 and got to the 970s and that was beginning to work as the 970s were starting to slow down and to get confused.

Then the clock interrupted my progress

All of a sudden the clock began to strike 11PM. It startled me out of my hard won almost-asleep-state just like an alarm clock might have done. I said to myself that since, for whatever reason, the chimes have given me this rude emotional shock, I'm going to use the shock as a hypnosis induction to put me to sleep. I did an Instant Back Relax and told myself that I would be asleep by the time the clock finished chiming. Well, I wasn't asleep at the end of the chimes but then I had another idea.

I decided to fool my mind into believing I was asleep even if I wasn't really asleep. I just kept insisting "I am asleep, I am asleep, I am asleep. Whatever thoughts I think are just dreams because I am asleep. Whatever sounds I hear are just dreams because I am asleep. I am asleep. I am asleep."

I must have momentarily lost consciousness as I was aware of dream images that had just occurred. I continued with my chosen thought."I am asleep. I am sleep." The thought "I am asleep" seemed to fill my entire mind. Other confused images started to arise and change shape."I am asleep. I am asleep." Odd dream-like images and phrases came up. I went to sleep. I did not hear the clock again and it chimes every half an hour.

EXERCISE #3: THE CLEVER ACCOUNTANT

We have to be very clever accountants, emotionally speaking. We should never, for instance, carry the failures of today forward into tomorrow. As we are preparing for bed, it is very easy to slide into the remorses if we have over-eaten. It's easy to beat ourselves up if we have taken some terrible social belly flop, haven't finished the report, or didn't get the house cleaned. However accurate these thoughts may be, it is simply not helpful in any way to think them. Thinking of a failure puts our brain in touch with an infinite amount of negative neuronal connections in our head (via learned association) which will just stress us out. Instead, we should keep carrying forward our successes, however small.

If we can't magnify some success in our mind, we should keep repeating the small things as a kind of positive-train-of-thought which can turn into the kind of thought-jamming to silence those insistent negative thoughts. Yes, maybe we didn't lose weight today but we lost two pounds so far this week. Yes, maybe we over-ate but there was probably some small thing we passed up. "Hey I didn't eat that third brownie. I was victorious over the third brownie. And anyway, it didn't taste really all that good. Maybe I'm getting tired of junk food. I'm losing my taste for junk food. I think I'm starting to want to eat better. Eat healthier." It's even a victory of sorts to say "Hey, I did over-eat, and now it's over. It's gone. I am free from what I did today forever because today is soon gone and thank goodness for that."

Our small triumphs don't have to make sense in the grand scheme of things or even in the grand scheme of our lives. They just have to be positive so that they will connect with other positive thoughts in our mind by learned association. This is really a mind trick like some bookkeeping is an accountant trick and doesn't make good mathematical sense.

It's the process that's important

If we have been really low functioning, it is a victory to have brushed our teeth or to have taken a shower. For those of us who are high functioning, perhaps we didn't win the Pulitzer this year but we have done the first chapter of our next book.

Don't forget that our pain is exactly the same whether we are high functioning or low functioning. So the victories, however small, can bring us equal emotional relief. The inherent importance of victories is not at all relevant. The *process* of being positive is more important than the *content* of the positivity. Brushing our teeth is no less positive than writing the first chapter of a book. It will have an equally positive effect, by learned association, with whatever positive mindsets exist in the neurons of our brain.

Not only are we connecting with the positivity in our mind instead of the negativity but we are forging another stronger positive neuronal pathway out of despair with every single good thought we think. We can follow-up chanting the litany of our small positive actions with the good old standby Emile Coue mantra. "Every day in every way I am getting thinner and thinner." "Every day in every way my house is getting cleaner and cleaner." "Every day in every way I am eating healthier and healthier." "Every day in every way my report is getting done-er and done-er."

As I said, the positivity doesn't have to make regular rational or grammatical sense to be a good mind trick. It just has to be positive. Sometimes if we get far afield we might even amuse ourselves and these little inside jokes are positive, too. As far as thoughts go, any class positive beats first-class negative.

EXERCISE #4: DEEPER AND DEEPER

In my hypnosis work I use the phrase "Deeper and deeper" all the time to further a person's relaxation. I use it for myself as well. I find that I have associated relaxation with these two words to such an extent that sometimes all my mind needs is to think some repetitive "Deeper and deeper" to get me right to sleep. As you use this phrase for yourself, you will also build an association to relax and get to sleep. Visualize, or sense your whole body falling heavily down, down into the dark as you think the words.

EXERCISE #5: PEACE BE WITH YOU: YOU ARE NOT ALONE

Another wonderful phrase for re-connecting is to say this phrase silently to your self, over and over. Think about particular people who may be troubled, struggling or ill, or even strangers. In giving peace to others you will be giving it to yourself as well. And if you say this for me, I will now say it for you, "Peace be with you. You are not alone."

Arline Curtiss
San Diego, California

Index